Honest Guide to Child Custody Visitation Schedules

Real-World Experiences, Ideas, And Examples of Divorced Shared Parenting Including 50/50 Visitation Schedules

Clay H. Emerton

What if you were inspired?®
Change Publishing, Atlanta

Honest Guide to Child Custody Visitation Schedules
Real-World Experiences, Ideas, and Examples of Divorced Shared
Parenting including 50/50 Visitation Schedules

Purchase the latest version at www.changepub.com
Change Publishing, LLC., Atlanta
www.changepublishing.com

ISBN 978-161510-001-9

Printed and distributed in the United States
First Edition

Change Publishing™
Sometimes beginnings...*Never End.*®

HONEST GUIDES
BOOKS & WORKBOOKS

A limited series of powerful publications produced by
Change Publishing, LLC.
www.honestguides.com

Honest Guides are written by authors who have intimately experienced and found practical solutions for life's most twisted complications. These publications are crafted to specific standards. First, a common problem must be clearly identified. Secondly, in the context of personal experience, the writer must provide a realistic solution to the problem. Thirdly, if the author cannot handle the issue in under two hundred pages, you won't find it in this popular series. A smaller, concise format allows the reader to fill in missing "fluff" resulting in a seriously *provocative* publication. Lastly, these publications are alive and breathing by reader participation. Through surveys and other methods of honest feedback, the writer and publisher can respond in highly anticipated revision.

During revision, the publication will maintain relevance by leveraging our *Four C's of Revision*:

> *Collecting and Responding to Feedback from Readers*
> *Current Event Illustration Updates*
> *Contextual Prowess- Recognizing Changes in Culture*
> *Conversational Language Use*

For Shauna.

Pretend

Pretend that I am the love of your life. Let's listen to Garrison Keillor at 10:30 AM on a Sunday morning, rain falling outside, windy, leaves blowing, in the fall. They are playing old timey music in between and telling stupid jokes about ketchup. I have on a tank top and flannel pajama bottoms. You have some sort of familiar feeling, like we have known each other forever. I can smell coffee, wet leaves, and that smoky camp-fire-in-the distance smell. I think that you are the best and you think that I am the most precious, even when I tell people off with conviction. Our conversation is not that deep, but we just know that we belong. You know that you want to be a part of me and me a part of you. This is a perfect moment in time. Let's pretend that Lake Wobegone really exists and that I am something worth protecting and living the rest of your life for.

-Nina L. Williams

ACKNOWLEDGMENTS (& INTRODUCTION)

*There are many who have contributed to the inspiration and to the content of this publication. Perhaps most influential have been my own loved ones, particularly those introduced below. In addition, I have been influenced by everyday conversations with other moms, dads, and even kids. Many have suffered with horrible child visitation arrangements. Changes start with **our** generation.*

*As an author, I do not expect you to agree with everything in this book. There are many controversial issues discussed and I understand that people learn truth as a personal process. While you will likely disagree with some or most of my positions on moral issues, political issues, and controversial social issues, you might be surprised with how much you eventually **do** agree with. As with anything, use what you can and leave the rest.*

FOR MOM

I appreciate *my mom, Vonda Kay Simpson.* Her positive influence reaches deeper inside my heart than words can ever express. My mom made it okay for her boys to express emotion, and as males growing up, this approach preserved more self-esteem than parents traditionally afford boys. She is everything I could want in a mom; however, in this book I have many unsavory things to say about her custody decisions during the early years of my childhood. I will never recover the lost memories that resulted from her choices, but *I understand* why she did what she did. Some might say that she had better options, and she did. Others might say that she made the best choices with what she was working with, and that would be true too. This type of situation prompts us to realize how "right" and "wrong" can be somewhat relative. Rather than calling her choices "wrong", I might interpret her decisions to lack "divine" perspective. When I speak of "divine", I mean the "most functional overall"; and even the word *functional* can be interpreted differently. In the end, we arrive to the ultimate problem: limited resources, especially time.

I still marvel at the amazing gap between my mother's options. She could have gone either way with how she handled her visitation situation. Knowing the laws and expectations during her custody crisis, only with divine-like intervention could better choices have been made. Governing these critical moments of decision are available resources, common ignorance, *practical* learning, and often, varying degrees of mental illness. The results are a multitude of butterfly effects, impacting children, other adults, and future generations.

I am thankful that my mom exchanged generous affection with me, even through adolescence. She has been nurturing, communicative, and interested in her children. Over the years, I have never wondered if my mother loved me, and that is a priceless awareness, often taken for granted by sons and daughters.

The scope of this book is appropriately considerate and perhaps narrowed by my relationship to **Richard Howard Emerton**, <u>my</u> father, who was removed from my *daily* life at a very young age. My writing also includes some divine experiences following *my own* divorce. I am an **equally respected** coparent to Kayla Lynne Emerton, Andrew Marcus Emerton, and Angela Kay Emerton. Just know that there is always more to any story, and as a reader, you need to respect that moms have the *completing* perspective. That perspective matters and is necessary to the provocative honesty within these pages. Much of what I have to say comes from the little boy still inside me who was hurt as a child.

FOR DAD

I appreciate my stepfather for his inspiration and his love. The achiever and diplomat within me took root and grew strong due to his uncanny leadership. While I was young, Larry Marcus Simpson shaped a world for me that made sense, and for that I owe the highest personal debt.

As inappropriate as it might seem, an acceptable acknowledgement of my stepfather will require an explanation of sorts. Since many Americans become emotionally disturbed when personally confronted with typical divorce law, my effort may be therapeutic for many daughters, sons, fathers, and mothers.

The explanation will require several pages, functioning as an introduction to this publication. The relentless impulse to explain my stepfather's situation is motivated by a deep desire to understand why his parenting abilities became increasingly limited throughout his adult experience. I want each of us to see the naked truth of what drives my thoughts and feelings about *typical* divorce settlements. To be honest, more than one "family court" facilitated the ruin of important family relationships during critical stages of my child development. Forensically explaining what has happened to parenting in America or explaining your own attitude about child custody almost mandates a critically evaluative approach. There is an enabling problem that I want to identify, and my stepfather's situation will establish our problem solving efforts.

Individuals involved in divorcing families are essentially vandalized, beyond valid repair, by our domestic legal traditions and social traditions. In all likelihood, even though I am going to warn you about it and explain it all in detail, you will walk right into the trap. Why is that? Perhaps because untold generations of folks have been handling divorce and post-divorce parenting in a way that will probably seem like the best option. In truth though, handling your divorce *correctly* would require unconventional awareness, relevant information, compassion, and a **significant** amount of personal fortitude. While you might *feel* like being in *survival mode*, the truth is that "survival" might involve more than a short-term approach. To the kids you are raising, to both parents involved, entire life experiences are at stake- beginning with individual maturity and ending with a sense of overall sanity (i.e.: personal mental and emotional integrity).

Like a modern smoker who eventually dies in a pathetic bed of cancer, you will know and see your poor choices unfold because you are probably not mentally and <u>emotionally</u> informed enough to protect yourself, your kids, and the man or woman you made babies with. People do not realize how gravely important emotional information is due to a tremendous amount of social conditioning and an imbalanced emphasis on intellectual education. The analysis and reconciliation of emotional information are rarely afforded the attention needed to properly resolve emotionally rooted malfunctions, especially inconvenient chemical addictions. Without statistical evidence, I assert that America's lack of emotional integrity has directly attributed to our unsuccessful struggles to reduce anxiety problems and substance abuse. Our imbalance also fuels a successful pharmaceutical industry to come up with "macho" solutions that don't actually correct the process that started the problem to begin with. It's like trying to drive a car without air in the tires. We arrogantly overlook the relevance and usefulness of basic air pumps because of the hassle and embarrassment involved in using them.

Feelings really *do* matter.

It is okay to cry. It is okay to admit we are weak and that sometimes we simply want to curl up in a ball of helpless feelings. It is okay to process our emotions and to determine what those emotions mean about our dysfunctional beliefs.

Why?

Our most difficult problems begin with unhealthy thinking patterns. Since these patterns are a consequence of faulty beliefs, emotions are useful at indicating when our beliefs might need closer examination. Even if we find that our beliefs seem aligned with all of reality's new information, the practice of acknowledging our emotions can help establish our identity and improve our sense of control over our lives. Emotional acknowledgement helps us develop the necessary infrastructure for advanced levels of maturity.

Personal and interpersonal emotional neglect can keep us held back without the tools we need to cognitively process many of the problems we individually face. There is a tension that remains indefinite and unidentified. Such tension will normally lead to humans who are unexplored, misunderstood and intuitively frigid to solve the most intimate problems.

Ask us to make a bomb? We can do it. Ask us to win a competition? We're there. Ask us to understand and acknowledge our vulnerable inner-child or to love another human being who seems different from us…and the country goes quiet. WTF are we supposed to do with that stupid idea? Inner-child? We are MEN! Wait a minute….umnnn we are men *and* *women* who all act like we have excess testosterone problems. We don't have to understand ourselves or anyone else because we are here to kick some ass; **anyone's** ass who gets in our way.

"God bless the USA!"

Some say that we only need Jesus to solve our issues when in fact, that conviction can sometimes permanently betray our ability to resolve serious problems. Why? Jesus isn't actually correcting the problems in our country. When was the last time an invisible god resolved your personal issues? As long as you believe that your problems are someone else's responsibility, nobody is actually solving anything. Some of you hate that I am offering my genuine feedback about this unfortunate dilemma. I do not take these statements lightly, but in **my** past experience, no matter how much I have permitted the grace of unmerited forgiveness and atonement in my life, my personal issues still haven't gone away until I actually work through them.

If Jesus is not going to sit down with us and work through our problems, then we might lose sanity if we depend on Jesus to do that. It is true that divine-like wisdom, patience, courage and forgiveness are typically essential virtues needed to effectively manage a divorce. The fact is though, you wouldn't be reading this book if god would simply jump in your head and explain all this to you. Your child custody situation will be one of the most important crossroads you will ever encounter, and left to normal devices, things don't look very good for you and your divorced family.

The path of your divorce is fairly predictable simply because the generic fuel of selfishness lends itself to the "surest" road. Since shared parenting is foreign to most divorcing parents and therefore, viewed as risky, many will not recognize that the unfamiliar road is actually the surest direction to take. I am just wondering if some information becomes most palatable in hindsight. *During* child development however, we find a dangerous period for adults to perform such trial-and-error learning.

This book is designed to provide you with information and outside perspective, so that you *might* make better decisions than your predecessors. My stepfather's situation is now a matter of history. It was very typical, and tragic. Something happened to him, his kids' mom, and ALL children involved in his life. Something that shouldn't have been acceptable to any informed facilitator, and yet it was. Allow me to illustrate his situation with an analogy.

When a child is molested or when someone is raped, others from the outside actually have to come into the picture to help the victim accurately process what has happened. The objective is to help the victim regain an accurate emotional and mental interpretation of themselves and the world around them. It seems like the sexual violation takes something healthy from someone, and without effective assistance, mental illness can consume a person. Sometimes the emotional and mental opportunities that a victim would have otherwise perceived are lost.

Not only this, those who has been violated feel a sense of embarrassment about the weakened state they perceive existed at the time of the molestation and by the fact that people feel like "helping" them. It is like adding fuel to the fire. Many victims would rather hide what has happened to avoid sympathetic attention. Those from the outside who learn about the crime are often beside themselves to see justice served. Meanwhile, the victim would rather hide the wound and move on if possible. "Why prosecute the wrongdoer? *Can't we just forget I said anything? Please just drop it!"*

Crimes that violate someone's sexuality do not stop at the initial trauma, do they? This type of personal violation can result in a lifetime of repercussions, with or without a victim even knowing how limited he or she has consequentially become. Severe penalties and the most <u>thorough</u> rehabilitation efforts are **necessary** for sex offenders.

For my stepfather Larry, I am stepping in for a moment to go on record about the **molestation** of his *parental identity*. I need to say some things that he should say. As a very forward thinker, perhaps he hasn't perceived the true relevance in dealing with water under the bridge. Since my present situation has been shaped by Larry's past, it's that older water I find so interesting right now.

I think Larry is a responsible man who knows his landscape well. In the present day, he appears to respect himself while he identifies and evaluates the real options in his life. After carefully considering choices and the potential consequences of the choices, he decisively makes the best possible selections based upon his priorities and ethical beliefs at the time. I have watched him live like this throughout his younger adulthood and still even today.

How hard it is for any dad or mom to integrate work, home, self-respect, and a culturally appropriate social identity? Personal ideological *success* is an expected goal of Americans; and yet, when we evaluate the process of maturity, it seems rather obvious that someone's parental growth will prove completely illusive if the actual role of being a *relevant* parent is removed by the **policing power of government**.

As a divorced American dad, I have to come out of my comfort zone to express my utmost disdain. Why are state governments rushing in to take away the daily parenting rights of any responsible parent? Your answer: *"Well, Clay, isn't it simple? It's because romantic relationships don't always work out. It's because marriages fail. It's because dads don't readily assume roles as responsible parents. In fact, they seem to shirk responsibility off on moms and claim that they are exempt from such efforts."*

How typically do romantic relationships actually work out?

How typically does someone outgrow a marriage?

How often are dads expected to take responsibility of kids?

The mere fact that a child has been conceived ought to be enough to get any man's attention. Somehow though, our culture has been confusing men to leave parenting up to females. This becomes most obvious when a man becomes unemployed or unsuccessful, since at that point, what good is he? I suppose such unnatural ideas are reinforced by those who make abortion appear as a *woman's* issue rather than an issue for both of the participants involved in human conception.

While perfectly fine to manage our romantic lives and our children prior to getting divorced, as dads and moms in this country, we are only certain of everyday admittance to the lives of our kids if we get lucky in romantic love or if we keep pretending to be happy in a contractual marriage. A step further, we can be *outright miserable* in a marital situation for our kids to witness and *learn from*, but so long as a separation or divorce doesn't reach the attention of the state, we are fine to keep the family in hell. What are we to do? Hand over our kids to the **mercy** of the state? Give up our ability to be dads or moms if something goes wrong in the impending custody battle?

Knowing the dangers involved, still sometimes, something *healthy* happens and a mom, dad, or couple will realize that a marriage is just not reconcilable with the interpersonal resources available. A light comes on about the brevity of life and the personal misery of continuing to entertain an unhealthy marriage. A divorce occurs. This is where it gets weird. The state government then steps in to decide who will be a real parent and who will be the backup parent.

I need to say something, and I need to be very clear on this: During a standard divorce, the state should always initially assume that the kids REMAIN in the full legal responsibility of **both** mom and dad in a **50/50 physical custody** arrangement. If temporary living situations are needed for 30, 60, or 90 days during the establishment of an appropriate second residence, then that is acceptable. If the state wants to make sure that parents establish and correctly execute a visitation schedule, then that is acceptable. However, kids should never be in the legal custody of ANY state for ANY reason other than actual criminal activity, and I am sorry, legislators, but divorce is not a crime unless you are a religious zealot— and if you are, what in the hell are you doing writing legislation that impacts my family in the typical sick way that religion historically can?

Remember when churches were segregated? Why was that again? Did the members of our churches impact our legislation at all? Or was it the legislation that impacted the churches? Was religion ever used to justify the segregation?

Marriage is not a noble option in and of itself. It is certainly romantic to consider marriage as a respectable alternative to single living or "shacking up." However, marriage can often be the outright stupidest legal, personal, and social decision a man or woman will ever make.

I was recently driving down I-75 here in Atlanta, and I looked up to see a billboard with a baby and a headline: *"Get Married and Stay Married- for the sake of the kids."*

THAT is exactly how I used to see things.

Then I actually got married and stayed married for the sake of the kids. The results were married adults who were sick, lethargic, and displaced from healthy independent thinking, and **with kids** who had *that* to emulate. Modern marriage is a preference and a personal choice due to the challenges to personal growth it will create. Marriage can provide many benefits, including a definite confrontation to our immaturities. Even "true-love" and caring families have to deal with the real world of limited emotional, mental, and physical resources. I frankly am not sure that 90% of those who marry have any idea what they are doing. Still though, it is *their* business, and they have the freedom to make such uninformed decisions—just like many of us have.

As an author, I will be working on separate projects dealing realistically with premarital considerations and active marriage. *This* publication will need to stay its course of child custody philosophy, legislation, and visitation scheduling. Just know that it is unrealistic to believe that I can fairly attempt a practical book like this without considering the context of American marriage.

People think that divorce is a type of personal failure. **I believe** it can also be a very interesting *success* if the post-marriage details don't get in the way. In truth, personal failures can be fairly relative and the entire concept of failure can be misused in our self-talk. The single most difficult feeling I had to overcome about my divorce was the feeling that I had failed and should have kept trying. I could have; and if *we* would have, it would have been the business of my ex-wife and me to continue dealing the shit we shoveled.

Doesn't *free-will* really provoke the social morality police with their hypocritical workaholic superegos? Am I going to burn in hell for getting a divorce? Let me burn then. Are my kids crushed by a dissolved legal contract? No. What about the fact that I have to rest my head on a different pillow at night? I think I can worry about raising my kids so long as people can keep their personal pet "family values" to themselves.

While divorce may not actually *fix* anything, it *does* provide an important function for families by preventing implosion or explosion when there are no other known effective solutions. The individual adults in a family determine if a solution might be effective or ineffective at solving marital dilemmas. With this knowledge, if legislators desire to see people make better marital decisions including the utilization of tools like marital counseling, advanced communication, sex therapy, etc., then such changes should probably start with additional interpersonal training during childhood education. High school, for example, would be an excellent time to provide our nation's future bride and grooms with brief introductions to unfamiliar professional resources. Once adults are already out making families, an intervention is often going to be too late.

The general experience of "romantic" love includes a special rule. That rule makes a woman or man feel like she or he is being forced into fixing something if that individual isn't already comfortable with using advanced resources. Basically, either married couples are comfortable with using professional tools going into a marriage, or they aren't and won't use the tools effectively. People who are coerced into using professional services like marriage therapy in order to fix their romantic problems will likely suffer. In her book *Against Love*, Laura Kipnis provides a hilariously sarcastic explanation of this phenomenon. If you need a good laugh about the frustrations of romance in marriage, you will find her book endearing and an intellectually outrageous page-turner. Some of you might also appreciate her book dealing with pornography.

Forcing a mom and dad to stay together, **never actually** works without one or both resigning into depression. My ex and I actually did try marriage counseling with a male therapist and then a female therapist; both were highly uninformative. Perhaps, there was nothing that could be done for us? Or were the therapists simply not ready to deal with a couple who wanted more than most therapists are willing to give? Maybe some therapists don't know how to live in the real world *themselves*.

I have recently wondered if those marriage therapists knew that Shauna and I would not stay married; however, to rush the divorce would have been a huge mistake. We had to reach such a conclusion on our own and that required months, if not years for us to determine. Couples cannot always see the writing on the wall when they *themselves* are part of the wall and the writing. For couples, sometimes the best solution is to take time seeking truth until it finally emerges. Realistic solutions for a unique divorce situation can also take time.

When considering family law, I find no place for the "do-good" manipulations from America's idealists. Such exceptionally caring individuals would be better situated to support improving our country's childhood education programs, or perhaps they might want to work in our nation's eye opening shelters for battered women—especially since typical big hearted idealists often unwittingly enable the social problem those shelters respond to.

I might be wrong on that last point. Am I?

Legislation needs to be developed by those who would recognize the grave danger in legislating *values* that not all individuals will fit or keep fitting. I am not talking about laws supporting abortion. Legislating abortion rights is not proactive, creative or intelligent. It is another way of **responding** to sick conservative ideals, rather than handling the real problems that make abortion seem necessary. I have to wonder if un-healthy legislation has been supported for so long in America simply to keep men and women *afraid* of realistic living. Being honest about reality is a clear *backhand* to religious tradition. Why let gay couples adopt children when such ideas are irreconcilable with popular religion? Better to abort babies then to have them with homosexuals (the *perceived* enemies of traditional family values).

◇ Why **remove** the shame from unmarried pregnancy?

◇ Why **remove** the shame from <u>married</u> moms who offer newborns up for adoption?

Such ideas make perfect sense, but not to people who are most concerned with playing games with human life by respecting asinine religious doctrine or suffocating social code. Many liberals and their closely related conservative bedfellows keep this strange compromise active.

☑ **Staying** *unhappily married* might actually *hurt children.*

☑ **Aborting** a pregnancy may actually end a human life (with a unique genetic code).

☑ **Pressuring** an overwhelmed family to raise *another* child might throw the family beyond its limited capabilities.

It seems that many of our elite legislators are convinced that Americans should be good Christians instead of being healthy adults who can reconcile reality.

"If a couple divorce in our state, the legal slaughter of that family will just prove our point that divorce is simply bad, wrong, and immoral. We will let each family disaster prove that divorce is bad because it wrecks families."

No, it doesn't.

While divorce can expose the individual financial vulnerability of either or both adult family members, it is actually divorce law, custody law, and cultural expectations that make the already difficult situation of divorce an emotional and fiscal bankruptcy every time. If we consider the serious problems with unexpected, unmarried and unwanted pregnancies, the issues appear even more complex.

When a state starts putting its hands immorally on our genitals, we need rescued. By doing things like stepping between two capable parents and "*awarding* rights" to the children involved, states have hands and fingers all over our parenting rights, the future opportunities of our children, and even our wallets. Women, by accepting child support in lieu of shared parenting, you are almost guaranteeing that you and your female peers will continue to be paid less than men. This may not be relevant in all situations, but there is a tremendous amount of truth to it, if you are honest.

Are you an honest person?

I want to unveil another dirty little secret. When a state divisively gets in the middle of a standard divorce, the entire family becomes thwarted from finding a safe point-of-balance, including mental and emotional reconciliation with the changes in mom and dad's marital status. At a confusing time when the family needs both parents the most, one parent is often removed from the area, leaving the alienated parent and the children to feel very insecure and helpless. It also permits far too much liberty for "the chosen" parent to manipulate the opinions of children about the divorce and the custody situation. It is NOT OKAY to support or allow legislation that supports the permanent removal of potential balance and accountability from a child's parenting <u>team</u>.

In the *twenty-first century*, our physical custody tradition is ABSURD!

I don't care about respecting tradition; I care about having morally honest, socially intelligent, and culturally relevant legislation *today*.

Let us not be naive. It is clear that enough financial stability is necessary to facilitate a home that might meet the basic needs of child-rearing. We must *also* be clear that our legal traditions have made use of this excuse beyond its shelf-life. Today, such traditional ideas are being executed in a way that clearly perpetuates other social problems. I do not submit that we sabotage financial *necessity*. Instead, I suggest that we improve our initial legal presumptions about typical divorced parenting visitation.

Responsible parents are capable of learning and supporting the morally ambiguous concept of a "child's *best* interest." Rather than dishing out sole custody decisions to save state resources, perhaps state governments should direct parents to select a **private**, licensed, family professional to unobtrusively verify the health of a visitation agreement. Maybe divorce education programs should be more focused in dealing with the needs of children *at different ages*. If states don't want to get this involved in divorces, then courts should mandate that parents work out the details of agreements, either privately or with mediators if needed.

When agreements are reached between divorcing parties, courts should then review the details of agreements to verify that details are enforceable by court order, and that is where the courts' social responsibilities end.

No custody battle is necessary because there is morally no place for such a "battle" to occur. There should be no legal vehicle for parents to arbitrarily fight for more than 50% physical custody of a child following the filing of a typical divorce. In addition, *legal* experts should not be making sensitive *family* decisions. Are the judges in all fifty states required to be experienced marriage and family therapists before taking their positions? If they are not, then why are they making decisions that inherently require skills outside of their professional training?

Clearly stated, the legal grounds for typical custody battles during divorce should be removed in all fifty states, most importantly because the current legal traditions are substantially enabling the minority status of American females, mothers particularly. The minority status of females adversely impacts all family members involved in divorce. It also corrupts potentially healthy relationships between male parents and children, starting from the moment of conception.

Consider a world where moms *don't* spend their lives in lousy marriages with only an alternative of single motherhood. How much more inspiring and engaging would moms be with their children? What if dads were obligated to take care of children in an alternating 50/50 schedule? America's corporations would then feel it necessary to accommodate kid schedules for **both** moms and dads.

Our current legislation has average and above average parents being reduced to treatment as incompetent at best, and like criminals at worst. WAKE UP. Do you smell what I smell? It's coffee. Are you awake? Let's sit down right now and discuss how we MUST set a purging fire through our state court systems—TODAY!

Let's start with some letters you can write to your state's political representatives in congress. You might even send a letter to the White House. It must be done **now**. The sick molestation of American families has gone on this long because people like me thought someone else was going to fix it. Guess what? They aren't fixing it.

If you give a damn about kids, moms or dads, then you must stop going through life pretending that politicians are looking out for you. Politicians are looking out for *themselves*, just like you do. Politicians work by perceived priorities, just like you do.

BECOME YOUR POLITICIAN'S PRIORITY.

Remember that your kids will soon be parents too, facing the same broken system. Your grandchildren will need both mom and dad if a divorce occurs, just like your kids do.

Admit it. Sometimes, in a culture of moderate education, limited resources, and unique persons, divorce is needed to effectively resolve our unique family identities. Family identity is naturally capable of absorbing an unhealthy marriage's dissolution. Once everyone has finally recognized what's happened, the <u>family</u> can then be more effective, even if mom and dad were not matched well for married life.

What in the hell is the state doing in the middle of *every* modern couple's romantic split? Monitoring the process to make sure that children are okay is fine, but to actively *participate* is unacceptable and should appall anyone with the slightest sense of personal autonomy, pride, and education. Our transitional social system is seriously lagging in its obligations; essentially betraying females and the maturing process that families *need* to experience—especially divorcing families who are actually admitting that there is a problem. If a logical and natural 50/50 custody arrangement is **the standard presumption**, then only one major event has occurred, and that is a formal breakup of two adults. Both of those people have the potential to be healthier *apart,* but were not healthy in a marriage together. Neither adult should be parenting alone.

Let's get back to my stepfather's specific situation. His kids were removed from his everyday life and he was "awarded" every-other-weekend visitation. Making the best of bad legislation was the Darwinian thing to do as a *seriously* alienated parent with limited rights. To be sure, admitting facts is crucial to personal mental health, and sometimes people simply have to admit that life is painful and move on. For Larry, parental molestation by the state removed realistic opportunities for him to mature as an engaging parent to his daughter and son. It also negatively impacted the maturing process for his kid's mom. Had Larry argued with the state, it would have been considered *more* harmful to the kids, but I think he should have done the wrong thing. He should have argued for 50/50 custody, no child support, and temporary alimony payments if appropriate. I am not aware of all the details behind his divorce situation, but I think every child wants to know that daddy would fight for a more balanced visitation schedule, regardless of the career costs and regardless of how dirty and manipulative the other parent might become.

I will not elaborate more about the unethical games that some parents play to keep control of child custody, though some of you know I could.

Had one variable been different, mental and emotional resolution for all members of Larry's divorced family would have eventually been available. The variable I speak of is the parenting assumption: true "shared parenting", rather than *single parenting,* would have changed *everything*.

Having said all that, Dad, thanks for doing the best you could to develop as a man and parent to Jennifer, Sean, Brandon, Cliff, and me. The holocaust our legal system put us through has you looking starved, head shaven; but you are still needed in the "everyday" lives of your children; just as you were needed throughout our childhood.

Dad, I believe you already knew all of the things I just wrote. I just thought I would go on record about my personal observations. There were many damnable facts that shaped your everyday life as an American father. I am grateful for your efforts to stay sane, to work with what you had, and to still be the best dad possible following a traditional American divorce crisis.

In your custody case, as with most cases, I know that **each** parent involved did whatever they felt was right at the time. I am simply not proud of our early years. It was a very inefficient use of your potential as a dad *with a family*. The laws *and social expectations*, being what they were, ultimately enabled the loss of very important opportunities you might have had, ***and that is not okay***.

These are the things you could process with more intensity, but perhaps you have no idea how therapeutic this sort of shit is, especially to your kids who suffered with you. Materialism and a career, in the end, are empty ways to express your natural ability to nurture. It's not the same as nurturing the real thing, but who could blame you? Isn't that what all the male readers of this book will probably do? Won't they follow the *divorced dad* script and eventually get caught up in obsessions with their careers and consumerism? The problem of course is that corporations and success, though important to social stability, are also based on business rules and those rules are without life or emotion. It's the classic struggle of capitalism- working with people who have emotional needs that a budget driven machine just can't compensate for.

Your personal relationships are taken to the grave too. That's all I am saying here. I have been circumstantially cornered to reexamine some things. Dad, maybe you should consider doing the same; although, as we know, it's your business to conduct your life as you feel best equipped, not anyone else's; and actually, that is the start of mental health...not the finish though. Proud males are everywhere, and they are mostly limited in their efforts to find "satisfaction". Have you found it yet?

FOR MY SIS

I appreciate my sister Jennifer, a mom of three children. She spent hours on the phone with me after reviewing the initial manuscript and her feedback eventually proved critical. Jennifer's values are much more traditional, but still, sometimes she is closer than a biological sister to me.

FOR THOSE WHO DATE *FUNCTIONAL* COPARENTS

I appreciate the lovers who spend their daily life with Shauna or with me. It takes someone special to deal with the fact that our kids' parents work tightly together, instead of against one another.

FOR MY KIDS

I appreciate my children for being patient as Dad and Mom perform our best efforts at parenthood. We are trying to establish enough security and enough freedom to give each of you an equal chance. We want you to grow into efficacious adults; adults who own their choices and the resulting landscape. One day (probably in your 30's or later), I expect the view to be as breathtaking for each of you as it has been for your mom and me.

FOR MY KIDS' MOM

Lastly, I am grateful for my enchanting coparent Shauna. She was my first bride. I was her first husband. When our children were infants, Shauna was a master builder in the loneliest hours. We experienced our share of drama, as divorcing couples can, but even now we are *still* trying to take care of our babies and ourselves. I hope the road of finding happiness and balance for our entire family continues strong. May the years bring us satisfaction for all we have struggled to nurture.

I remain deeply regretful that I didn't understand your struggles as a young mom. I was on a silly path leading to nowhere.

FOR MY READERS

To my readers? Thanks for the opportunity to have your attention. I expect that this publication will change your life; for the sake of your kids, I'm counting on it.

Honest Guide to Child Custody Visitation Schedules

Real-World Experiences, Ideas, and Examples of Divorced Shared Parenting including 50/50 Visitation Schedules

Clay H. Emerton

What if you were inspired?®
Change Publishing, Atlanta

FOREWORD BY MY KIDS' MOM

When Clay first asked me to review this manuscript, I was immediately cautious. What if I disagreed with the book entirely? As I progressed through the material, I realized exactly how important this one little book might be for so many divorced or divorcing couples. I do not always agree with what Clay has to say on everything, or how he sometimes words things, but I need to admit that on this one, I agree with him 100%.

I am raising three children with Clay, and we have come a long way on journeys of self-discovery and parenting. I listened to this man sob on the phone, trying his best to maintain composure as he tried to explain the project to me. This topic is sensitive; it's personal, and it's very close to our hearts.

Our divorce occurred within ten years of our honeymoon. Yes, we did start as a younger married couple, and we made a lot of mistakes. To be honest, we still do. It has not been an easy road to say the least, but somehow, in all of it, it's been worth the costs.

Take your time to consider the practical ideas here and especially his experience as a child of divorce himself.

I hope you find your own difficult journey to be just as rewarding.

Shauna L. Emerton

TABLE OF CONTENTS

CANDID THOUGHTS FROM MY KIDS' DAD

If you purchase this publication five years from now, it will not be the same. The 2009 release that you are currently reading is designed to be relevant to the *current* state of American parenting, which includes how we legally handle divorce.

THE FUTURE OF DIVORCE FOR YOU AND YOUR KIDS

I hope you are not going to experience divorce anytime soon. If you are, you should be afraid right now because the family court system is broken. You probably think that there is a morally safe road ahead, but the fact is that there really isn't. Any success would require that you take an unorthodox approach and that is not normally what people do. Unorthodoxy can make us uncomfortable due to the embarrassment or discomfort of working against the grain. Many of us do not like the uneasy feeling of standing our ground by telling others that we are right, making them wrong. That's why most moms and dads will just stick with typical legal norms, though these norms are actually designed to accommodate one of America's varied social crimes. The way *future* Americans handle divorce will not look the same. Once you fully grasp this issue and more importantly, the solution, you can team up with others to fairly update family law, first by state, but federally if necessary. I promise to rework this book after we fix the problem.

I think that American's have become *lazy*. Perhaps this is the wrong way to approach things. I don't normally use the word "lazy" because it is almost always used to insult someone or to negatively manipulate a person's behavior. I hope all of us cringe when we hear an adult call a child *lazy*. In truth, Americans are purely and simply, unmotivated.   Perhaps our current condition of complacency is the natural result of labor from others. Certainly we were once a nation led by intellectual rebels. Our leadership thrived on defending individual freedom from unjust, corrupt government. As a result, the caves of reason slowly became brighter; though somehow with the **darkest** corners.

Who now is willing to intelligently solve our remaining compromises of human liberty? Regardless of how the problems originated, are the weak links in our social chain to be apathetically overlooked? How much longer are we to postpone action?

Silence.

Courage to change; faith in others; and willingness to trust humans inspired. These are the tools of social brilliance; the guiding forces towards new potentials; eventually transforming the future of a people.

If appropriately equipped, would today's minorities not count costs and rise to challenges just as other have? What was the initial cause of the oppression? How are such messes undone without causing further *long-term* damage to those victimized? Are there risks involved?

Are there not *always* risks in human dealings?

Larger picture solutions **clearly** require courage, and courage is born in need. Today, the stakes are higher than ever. Consider the global nature of how societies currently influence one another. An exponential quality exists in how well Americans manage social responsibility (i.e.: human mutuality).

Right now, many American leaders realize the historical errors in our tendency to create and exploit minorities. Though this awareness exists, reform has impossibly been depending on pressure from the populous and the broken. With unintelligent principles governing change, anyone wanting a faster end to the darkness recognizes the unsolvable equation.

A prime example is the length of time our nation has wasted grappling with ignorant stratification sanctions on someone's skin color. Affirmative action has been a **necessary** tactic for turning the tide on our country's *white male* tyranny. To be historically fair will require that Americans admit something: It has typically taken untold generations to aggressively correct minority oppression.

Why?

To what god shall we blame, or bow to, as explanation?

Perhaps my best example of minority oppression is much closer to home. Today, we watch a powerful *majority* who appear content with continuing to allow the mishandling of yet *another* minority, a social class who has been conditioned for generations to accept being tossed around like ragdolls.

I am referring to American females.

I have two daughters, and this problem worries me. While at one time I had considered feminism to be a threat to America, as a father I have come to realize that, in fact, the traditional American way of life is a threat to my daughters. My girls deserve and will be encouraged to DEMAND equal opportunities to learn and use their talents and passions. I don't want them thinking that they should skip college to stay at home with kids; and it is not that I don't think my daughters should change diapers; instead, it is that the notion that my girls should be stuck changing diapers *alone* is completely primitive.

Marriage and parenting **are** very convenient to bundle. However, the truth is that my first marriage taught me that the real world is not always *convenient*. Some of you need to get your heads out of your asses long enough to witness what is all around you. Right now, in your country, *females* are treated very oddly by our legal system, and for problematic reasons.

My daughters **do not** need to be the *only* ones taking care of children. We need legislation and family courts to reinforce the idea that a man who impregnates one of my daughters will be joining in the *fun* of parenting **with the *same* time commitment**. Single fathers, including divorcing fathers, should be expected and legally mandated to make **equal** investments of time, work, and finances—from changing diapers to helping with schoolwork. Writing a child support check doesn't constitute parenting.

The divorced or single dad to one of my grandchildren will be far from alienated. This is because my daughters are capable of supporting themselves while *splitting* childcare expenses and responsibilities.

No child support. No custody battle.

Neither of my girls should have the arbitrary ability to assume primary physical custody of a child since there is another parent involved; a very necessary parent. A divorced dad to one of my grandchildren will need a suitable home to sustain responsible childcare 50% of the time, plus pay for his share of diapers, formula, clothing, and other expenses. In such a circumstance, one of my daughters should not be encouraged to freeload off of another human simply because she has been impregnated by him. That other human is a parent and should be respected as a parent.

Pay attention to this point. Our American daughters will eventually have fair earning opportunities if more Americans would stand behind legislation that effectively corrects the unfair wage gap between genders. Most realistically, **if our domestic legislation and court tradition were to stop treating moms like they are only good for homemaking, fixing the wage discrimination problem would require fewer compensation lawsuits.**

Are you hearing me? God I hope you are.

It will probably take a miracle for some of you to leave your blissful spots of glazed-eyed ignorance. More than likely you will simply have to die and be replaced by other humans; humans who will naturally be positioned with greater mental freedom; and perhaps more common sense. Preconditioning has its uses to control crime and encourage peace, but it can also be an unfortunate shepherd of open-minded development. Few people are able to overcome the mental captivity of *predecessor design.*

Additionally, I suppose an activist's challenge, like mine right now, is to balance a position of social courage without being alienated as a freak or attention clown.

Didn't my daddy give me enough attention?

No. He didn't.

Staying back to consider the activist, we have the whole of society. Poor, rich, smart, or lucky, humans define various *lines of conduct* (paths to "success") and then take position in line. While walking or running in such lines, people shift between moments of boredom and amusement.

Are you entertained now?

Currently, our individual state legislatures seem to be okay with allowing women to continue a trend of *dependence on men* for monetary provision while assuming *grossly* imbalanced domestic duties. It is not healthy for mothers, their lovers or their children. Respect begins with mutuality, and mutuality begins with fair domestic expectations. *Functional* love between two domestic partners cannot exist without individual respect, which includes the capability to support oneself both emotionally and physically. Most folks have love perverted into something sick. So long as love is expressed between **opposite** genders, people think that it will all work out no matter how unfair the situation is.

By the way, I find homosexuality to be normal. Just because I am not gay doesn't mean that I should define the homosexual lifestyle as unnatural. It may not be natural to me, but that doesn't mean it isn't natural for you or others. If there is anything that's natural, it's the expression of sexuality and most importantly, a human's ability to select the most suitable companion. By suitable, I mean comfortable. By comfortable I mean *natural*. Silly arguments about vagina's and penises are irrelevant. Why in the hell is it your business to worry about whether a couple can biologically have kids or not? Oh I forgot. God made it your business right?

No dumbass. God certainly hasn't made another human's personal life your business. I am certain that through someone else's poor leadership, you have inherited this habit of jumping into other people's private lives. Maybe you have heard someone claim that it's okay to interfere with another person's freedom when the person has done something against your religion. Oddly enough, you use the same personal freedom to choose an "approved" sexual partner and since you are most comfortable with someone of the *approved* gender, you are free from the judgment of modern America's pharisees and sadducees.

Do you believe that judging others is fine when dealing with homosexuality since it's "everyone's business" to correct such a transgression? Do you feel like you will be held accountable for someone else's personal life? The logic of your religion isn't really logical at all is it? Oh but only with faith as a child can someone enter into the kingdom of heaven. So logic doesn't apply right? It's all about faith in things that don't reconcile with reality or faith wouldn't be required, right?

Faith "as a child" has <u>nothing</u> to do with the context of this section. Your lack of hermeneutical consistency when handling the scripture of your own religion is more shameful than the sins you regularly commit in private. If you were fairly interpreting the entire bible, I believe we wouldn't be having this conversation at all; though not for the reasons you think I might imply.

Am I making you tense?

This is why religion causes war. I will probably receive death threats and my children could lose a father simply because some religious zealot believes that I am working for satan. Scary isn't it?

Get back in line Mr. Emerton…with the rest of god's people. **Or else.**

The way popular America has handled homosexuality illustrates my point about how our culture restrains capable citizens in very dark corners. The most powerful and accepted crowds, though perhaps less capable, unintelligently **guard** the bulk of our country's power and resources.

While individual competitiveness is certainly reasonable, it is not smart for us to restrain capable people unless we want to compromise our strength as a nation. Why would we want to do that? What purpose would be served?

I think some Americans are so arrogant that they just can't fathom how these outdated social habits could, and *already* are leading us into very bad places. Around the corner is the potential for compromised economic strength which could lead to enormous national security risks. We are one major event shy of having children who don't have basic needs met like food, water, shelter, clean toilets, education and healthcare. Arrogance is for fools who will fall hard. Might we instead choose a healthy and balanced *confidence* based upon intelligent management of social resources. When we recognize modern challenges like global warming, it should be apparent that obtaining realistic answers will prove impossible if we are instead worried about food and shelter for our families.

On a lighter note, homosexuality illuminates individual immaturities within homophobes. While homophobia is not recognized as a personality disorder, I think homophobic feelings and related discrimination are mostly caused by deficiencies in one's intellectual and emotional capabilities. Those who would attempt to force or shame other adults into heterosexuality appear the most challenged to love another human being deeply.

Think about it.

WEAK FEMALES CAN'T SUSTAIN ROMANCE

Romance can last if it grows between two independent and mentally healthy individuals who <u>don't</u> actually *need* each other. They should *want* to engage each other instead and that is a **huge** difference.

Nationally, while it certainly is the right of Americans to maintain racial and gender oppression as *personal* pets, much like some people keep their mean little Chihuahuas, *it is <u>not</u> okay* for our court system to support these problems.

By the way, I have a Siberian Husky. Your Chihuahua would eat my dog for breakfast, so you and your little rodent can stop barking now.

The remainder of our text presents an interesting perspective about this nation's criminal pastime of oppressing women and then asking these same females to smile and shake their heads in modest approval. After all, isn't that what being a woman is all about? Smiling, overcoming frigidity, and being "sexy" while taking care of all the things men don't want to handle.

Right.

The problem with our legal way of handling divorce has often been considered an issue against men. In truth, it has always been a reinforcement tool enabling the oppression of females, especially moms. This publication will deal a lot with this issue because it has to. It is scary that our culture passes down the asinine belief that "men are where the strength stays."

Excuse me?

Just because the manifestation of strength between genders is *different* does not actually mean that one gender should rule over the other. Men and women are naturally equipped with unique hormonal potentials, and such differences can allow variants in behavioral patterns **when** circumstantial freedom permits.

In which enchanted neon port-a-potty are people entering and then stepping out to declare that the differences in gender are cause for *Mom* taking care of the kids almost totally alone, married or not married? By the way, when a child is asked to give up routine contact with either parent, marital status is <u>not</u> so important. Marriage seems to matter to religious folks and other preconditioned agents of our society. Kids on the other hand, are innocently less concerned about the way we socially stratify parents and families.

Clear differences in the genders can be appreciated without grossly misinterpreting the meaning of those differences. It is not *at all* necessary to encourage, reinforce, or otherwise support the exclusive right of men to control the bulk of our country's economic resources and political power, especially when moms are frequently stuck with lower paying employment while still being expected to function as the primary "maker" (i.e. worker) of the home. There was a time when women were treated *so* unfairly, that they were excluded from owning property. *Conveniently*, they were also not legally allowed to vote. A female back then that dared buck the system was socially brutalized as a threat or worse, a witch.

No, the *human* who rebelled against the obviously unjust system was not evil. She was not strange either. The female "rebel" was simply sidestepping unfair expectations on her, like a healthy human **should**. She was brave, but others would label her *insane* or delusional for not staying in line with the other slaves.

Was she insane? A slave? Am I taking this a little too far?

Actually, I am not going too far, but only someone who has already taken the time and brainpower to test these ideas for validity would be jumping off a chair right now in agreement. These ideas are not new; many have known about female oppression for much longer than you probably want to acknowledge.

A basic, young, run-of-the-mill white male *is able* to see it?

I do see it now.

COMING OF AGE

There was a time when I feared and even hated men and women who perceive what I do today. I thought that people like me threatened the families of America with liberal nonsense. Of course, back then I didn't actually develop my own beliefs based upon historically observable facts. Instead, I just copied the ideas of my conservative parents, my pastor, or even popular media personalities.

I was living a rather empty life, because I was afraid of high-altitude truth. Once willing to admit that most of the moral information I had been taught was *potentially* inaccurate, _honesty_ rather than *loyalty* became a part of my belief system. Let me reword that. I became loyal to recognizing truth, even if such loyalty compromised my approval rating with other personalities-even good old dad. In the end, I was rewarded with the discovery of a new interpersonal tool: full-range intimacy with reality.

I began to understand the interactive, big picture process behind current reality. I also began to perceive the influences of variables involved in reality as it actually emerges. A paradigm…evolved.

Question authority.

AMERICA'S TREASURED TRADITION OF LOVE

People can indeed be friendly, warm, and caring, <u>all</u> while being sincerely wrong in matters of social policy. By *wrong,* I mean dishonest. By *dishonest,* I suggest that people of power tend to secure power by skipping important facts. They then apply priority on tradition instead of applying it to the health of individuals. In fact, many American's seem to believe that by following tradition, no matter how dysfunctional individuals might become, a natural atonement for the tradition's weaknesses will magically occur. This is frequently the logic used when young adults approach *marriage*: get pregnant and married, but not necessarily in that order. Somehow, with a ring, some vows, and a baby, everything will work.

"Were gonna be so happy!"

Such tradition is often **encouraged** by social authorities *including* parents, religious leaders and even the popular media. It is *wrong* for not being factually inclusive and for not being healthy to the individuals involved.

Love is not a ring, or vows, a feeling, or a matter of character.

"Love" is not really what makes marriage work either. Some have suggested that less than 5% of couples who marry will later consider the marriage to be "highly satisfying." Just because love is apparent within uniquely satisfying marriages, doesn't mean that love is the magic. I assert that love sometimes exists *in spite of* marriage, especially apart from marriage, and not actually *because of* marriage.

The peculiar conception of *lasting* romantic love requires natural enablement through basic factors involving shared goals, comparable needs, chemistry in cognitive reasoning, and compatible maturity. So in fact, the true ingredients used to cultivate satisfying love and lasting romance might appear somewhat "unromantic." The typical inexperienced fool will almost always rely on popular culture's idea of *love-by-marriage* as the easiest way to romantic satisfaction.

An experienced eye can see that marriage is not erotically romantic or sensually appealing. Marriage is in fact a legal position with a state government and perhaps a tool to help people win social points with friends. At worst, marriage can become a tradition of delusion and manipulation, eventually leading to various personal malfunctions. In America, the demise of a marriage will typically lead to an unthinkable *physical separation* of children from parents.

Marriage and love exist as autonomous experiences- but they <u>do</u> appear **simultaneously** *on occasion.* Perhaps I am saying that marriage should be the formalization of something already known between two friends, and yet most often it is considered to be a substitute for genuine friendship. The tradition of marriage takes over *people,* rather than having any real, long-term utility.

AMERICA'S TREASURED TRADITION OF SUPERGOD

This same principle applies everyday to our families when dealing with religion. Look, an individual family member's emotional and mental health is far more important than the tradition of church attendance, prayer and any other measurement of religious compliance. The fact that anyone would backwardly imply that god would want mentally unhealthy followers boggles my mind, but that is what some people believe <u>without</u> saying they believe it. Am I a bad man for bringing it up? Is it tasteless? Should we sweep such unhealthy beliefs under the rug?

It's time we all got honest.

All of life's issues can be solved by attending church and praying, since an all-powerful god helps the faithful disciple.

Right?

Right.

Drop that theory, and some of you could stop reading right now; consider the thoughts presented already, and walk away with much more satisfying lives, divorced or not; lives free of obviously unhealthy bondages to social tradition. This book is not designed to blindly change your beliefs. That wouldn't be healthy at all and would only continue a *bahahahaha*ed habit of yours. The length of the book and the style of writing are designed to leave you to ***your own*** personal conclusions- which may take time to work through.

Look at your religion closely. A personal, **all-powerful** god may not fairly reconcile with reality. I was raised within the same Christian culture. I even went to bible college. To be completely transparent, I admit that I will probably never deny that many Christian tenants are philosophically desirable to me. However, currently I am asking how an omnipotent deity *who loves mankind* can exist when I still have to account for concepts like innocence, ignorance, and mental illness. When I include facts like child cruelty, pediatric medical misdiagnosis, and child suffering in general, I am stumped to explain how the world and the traditional American god can exist together in harmony. For the apologists, I *already* understand the theological tenant of "original sin." I am familiar with many theological defenses of Christian doctrine. At this point in my life, I honestly find the arguments completely inadequate.

As a compelling philosophical gimmick, a loving and powerful *supergod* is traditionally acceptable to Americans, and was to me for years. I now strongly believe that introductions to unconditional love are sometimes needed to help us compensate for inadequacies we might have suffered during child development.

Why is religion important to this book?

It's because I have to understand my own culture, my own conditioned perspective and my functional treatment of the traditions I often blindly treasure. To be fair to your children, you would be wise to do the same.

When reviewing your ideas about parenting, you might discover that some of those ideas may not be accurate when all facts are accounted for; especially the facts dealing with gender roles. Many people simply and blindly share a collective belief that tradition is more important than the *people* who follow the tradition. Reread that statement and notice that it should disturb all of us.

Enter: *Deadly and exploitative legal systems, complacent citizens, typical politicians, and persuasive religious leadership.*

Don't forget the nature of consumerism. There are many commercial possibilities when dealing with vulnerable buyers. Gotta get your official one-true-religion tee shirt before strapping on the bomb or drinking the Kool-Aid.

"Go Team Allah!"

"Jesus Rules."

Inevitably we arrive at: *"Let's kill us some infidels."*

Normally, religions lose relevance if they cannot first leverage the current ignorance, intelligence, and psychology of the masses. Maybe you, normally bored by history, disregarded or forgot about the historical legal struggles of women. It is possible that you have not been motivated to connect your present attitudes with laws that basically said women were incompetent to exchange resources with men. Have Christian churches historically debunked such a belief, or reinforced it? There are a significant number of Americans today who rely on an arsenal of bible verses defending the position that women should cook, clean, stay home and stay married, *or else.*

Are such beliefs really honest?

Though people might word their beliefs differently, or try to pad such beliefs with politically correct dialogue, essentially many people nurture the oppression of females at the core of their domestic values. Even females do it. I can remember taking a psychology class in high school and learning about how black children used to want white dolls over the black dolls. Why?

MOM, HAVE A COCKTAIL

Now, some of you actually thought that this problem of female oppression was resolved back when women were *given* rights to vote. You thought that men were not smart enough to keep control of things once females had the power to select American leadership. I submit that tradition has found ways to keep the prior conditioning alive for much longer than anyone could have ever imagined. In 2009, females are using only 16.8% of the 535 congressional House and Senate seats. Woman can vote right now. Why is each branch of our government still looking like a sausage fest?

When considering American families, your kids will one day scoff at how pathetic it was for women to be stuck with outrageously unhealthy custody arrangements. Females have been robbed of independence, while dads have been encouraged to buy their way out of fatherhood through paying something called "child support."

And everyone has gone along with it.

Nothing changes until something changes in between your ears. As a nation, we must question tradition, or become a pawn of it.

For those of you experiencing a divorce right now, I know you might be hurting, and I will help you get some things organized. Initially though, you really need all of your marbles available so that a successful position can be established for you, your coparent, and your kids.

I am going to continue leveraging rhetoric, personal experience, and an analytical approach to cultural ideology. Why? To help you buck hard against the outdated and ignorant family court system. I am going to encourage you to be responsible instead of accepting the pacifier of your parent's generation.

We have a social situation right now that prompts females to **forfeit integrity** by either staying in bad marriages due to fear and guilt, or by clearly taking kids from natural fathers while accepting the role of *Single Mom*. Meanwhile, Mom is being encouraged to expect up to 30% of a father's income only to eventually remarry and use up to 2.3 incomes to support only one household. The *entire* divorced *family* senses that the kids should be with their father a lot more; yet the expectations on a father are to provide money, and then be guilt-tripped for not having the kids more often. This guilt trip occurs conveniently AFTER Mom has allowed Dad to feel like a glorified grandparent instead of a father. She starts seeing him walk away and then suddenly realizes how the situation has impacted Dad's parental psychology. But it's too late. In the present situation, often America's dads can't reconcile the fact that their wages are garnished and that they feel like a convenient sitter for Mom- the **real** parent.

More often than you might think, dads are emotionally abused in order to finance an unfair physical custody tradition. Our culture's mishandling of a male's time to physically parent children produces a series of inadequate coping mechanisms, further destroying the potential for effective parenting and feeding the overall situation.

Moms normally don't want to parent children alone. Eventually they might even realize that a break from the kids is wanted and sometimes, needed. Dad is often broken more than Mom could have ever imagined. He appears less responsible and disconnected. She doesn't understand what happened to him. How can he be so distant? Why is he less interested in parenting his kids?

What a low-life he turned out to be!

No wonder you divorced him.

Is he really a loser? Did the divorce custody situation alienate him somehow?

It is a guilt and depression *cocktail* for many Moms.

Our latest president recently signed legislation making it easier for females to sue corporations. What for? Wage discrimination. Moms, I am not sure if you know it or not, but you really needed that.

POWERFUL PARENTS NEEDED

This book is very personal to me. I address the child custody issue as best I can with an admittedly limited perspective. In fact, I am looking forward to improving my own understanding of the topic by listening to your feedback. Perhaps by hearing your personal experiences, revisions to this publication and exceptional social accountability can be made possible. The goal is twofold, first, to make your situation easier to understand, and second, to make a better parenting situation for tomorrow's parents and children.

I am not a father's rights advocate. I am not a feminist either. Both of those groups have some really great ideas and some *seriously* bad ideas and frankly, I venture to say that *some* individuals in groups like that are simply interested in winning a fight or having a purpose. I already have plenty of purpose, yet I am interested in seeing increased opportunities for moms, dads, and especially kids.

I want moms to be *powerful* moms, dads to be *powerful* dads, and kids to have increased opportunities for rich, nurturing childhoods. Having two separate homes is indeed odd, and even cumbersome. However, following a divorce and having one home, with *only one* parent present, is an empty ship at sea to a child--*way* out in the depths of gray where nobody can hear a son or daughter crying for the other parent; drifting into developmental hardship.

I have lived in that gray as a child, and the emotional pain was excruciating. And it wasn't because of the divorce itself, but because my mom and the court seemed to discard my other parent without fair regard for my sibling, my dad, or myself.

As a six–year-old, I remember feeling like it was very strange when Dad moved out of our home. It didn't break my heart though, until my father began to follow the court mandated every-other-weekend visitation schedule. Almost immediately following the official custody decision, my mother relocated us. As a result, several lives were never the same again.

Divorce doesn't mean that one parent has to disappear except for every other weekend. I am divorced, but my kids still have both parents, so <u>you tell me</u> how that is possible. My kids are not lost, nor are their parents; and I live deep in the bible belt, in a conservative state that believes parents are probably idiots for having kids and getting divorced. **You tell me why my kids are fine and why divorce didn't destroy our lives.**

The answer is obvious: The coparents who take care of my kids had to adjust our beliefs and our values to match reality, and as a result, mental health emerged in our family. A divorce was needed. A division of parents from kids was not included in the divorce since our kids didn't divorce anyone.

Bing.

HAVING THAT CAKE

Do you understand that much of depression is actually due to your inner struggle to maintain ideal values in the face of life's facts? You can't argue with facts unless you want to start showing signs of mental illness. If you make your values *nonnegotiable* with reality, while perhaps romantic, you will end up spending much of your life wishing that things were different. You should not stubbornly refuse to adjust your values when you notice that they can't stand alone. In fact, if you are interested in achieving stretching goals before you die, you are going to need beliefs that are a little more durable to the cold rain and hot sunshine of life.

The careful nurturing of traditional family values can be an appealing sport for many of us. However, a coming-of-age should still occur when we finally face the honest facts of what our family courts are seeing: Americans are frequently not staying married. Our nation's newlyweds hope to stay together forever and I am sure that such hope fuels many industries to reinforce the idea further. The fact remains that hopeful marital ideals have some of the worst odds. Couples don't stay together by might or by wishing. They stay together by being circumstantially compatible.

You don't want to hear what I have to say about marriage. Some of you think I am taking divorce too lightly. For those readers who look at my divorce and want to tell me how to be successful in a future marriage (since I obviously don't get it,) please get back to me after you work through the infidelity in your relationship. Come back with a valid assessment of how the affairs happened and what they mean. I might listen to you when you have something interesting to say, something original- even personal. I am done with the ideal and now **I want honesty**.

Tell me how you reconcile the full facts of what you have with want you really want. I am 100% convinced that when most Americans are totally honest with themselves, they tend to want paradoxes- to have cake, and to eat it. Somewhere in the space between having that cake and eating it is where the problems start. I cannot speak of what a *wise* American might want. It would be hypocritical of me to try.

The human condition must be accounted for.

A MATTER OF LAW

Why people aren't staying married is <u>not</u> the central problem of this book, nor is it a court's job to learn. Courts should enforce your state and federal laws. That's it. Divorce law should do one thing. It should insist that a couple negotiate their own fair divorce, or if they can't do it alone, they should involve a mediator to have a fair divorce negotiated for them. The negotiation should initially assume a 50/50 custody arrangement unless very relevant information is presented to suggest otherwise. If *relevant* information *is* presented involving one parent who wants equally shared physical custody but is unfit due to drug or alcohol problems, violent offences, etc., the system should immediately require a licensed family therapist. An experienced professional can determine what training or treatment might correct the "fitness" of either parent. In other words, a realistic *divorced-family* plan should be created and executed and it needs to acknowledge both parents.

That's it. No custody battle. No trying to *prove* someone is unfit. Our laws normally contend that a child's best interests are important. While this is true, such ambiguous language leaves a little too much room for one legal expert to ruin parent-child relationships.

Parents who are disappointed, selfish, uninformed, or hypocritical typically emerge from custody battles and **you** need to help America put a stop to it. The fact that a parent is an ignorant racist redneck, a flag burning liberal activist, or a homosexual, has nothing to do with "fit", unless you are to play god with American parenthood, which wouldn't surprise me if you tried. It's easy to play god when god isn't around to backhand your ass.

Is government protection *ever* needed? <u>Yes</u>. We need to have the police and other government agencies intervene when domestic abuse occurs. I also believe it is our social responsibility to help prevent domestic abuse from happening in the first place.

Let us not make *all* families require government manipulation. Right now, in America, that is exactly what happens when a regular family lands in divorce court. Such legal manipulation is less than appropriate. Considering a compromise, I wonder what would happen if moms and dads redirected the cash currently funneled to attorneys. What if the money instead went to a standard divorce intervention? Not an intervention to prevent the divorce, but to assist with a satisfactory post-divorce parenting plan. Would America's domestic issues and criminal system clean up quicker? Nowadays, one divorcing parent gets offered a gift, wrapped by our legislation. The court's gift is a family-sized coffin.

If this is true, why is deficient state law remaining unchanged when the law is harming children and parents?

I have already answered that question. You simply did not want to acknowledge the simple truth of the answer. Why not? Because you actually still believe that women belong at home with babies. Inevitably, you also maintain a separate but necessary belief: Dads belong on the job with the real freedom. What kind of freedom? A dad can totally debase the traditional American mom's pitiful existence, simply by doing one thing: leaving her.

It is the core of the problem.

STRONGER FEMALES WANTED

Effectively, women have been presumed as lesser people than men, perhaps even less trustworthy. It's a total sack of cowshit. While you might thing my tact is tasteless, I find your values far more tasteless. Traditional "family values" are a sack of interdependent lies that don't really function because both mom **and** dad need to be *fully deployed* individuals. Currently, divorce begs a question: Is Mom healthy, capable, trained and trustworthy to take care of herself if needed?

I think that Mom just needs to be *more* of a woman instead of being limited to domestic duties. Sometimes, matters are confused *even more* by the men involved. Men should step aside and stop thwarting female autonomy. It seems that some men are insecure; scared of healthy females, when, in fact, two *obviously capable* partners are needed to **sustain** passionate companionship, amazing romance and increasingly erotic sex. Not only that, for Americans to enjoy diverse and balanced families, corporations, politics and national defense, it is critical that females become more involved in **everything**. American males appear mentally deficient when accepting and enabling female oppression. How is that "sexy" to them? Personally, I begin to grow bored of the typically reduced female. Her social compliance (or complacency) is not admirable, but in fact boring. I feel the pangs of discomfort when I realize that she is only a product of her country's making. If you have recognized the negative consequences of this phenomenon personally, it probably breaks your heart as it does mine.

Female intelligence and beauty attract me. I am not different from other men by such enamorment. I am admittedly awestruck by the naturally miraculous prenatal miracle. However, once these tickets have been redeemed, the truth is that there must be more. I feel that a woman should bring engagement to the table, not submission. And, ladies, you couldn't have kids without sperm, and men had no control over the fact that pregnancy selected the female gender rather than a male's. Both genders work with the way things are.

I am not reducing our differences either, but I am asking about the *other assets* that American females might exchange with their society. Mom, Dad, do you have a college education? An education opens up whole new doorways of understanding using a profoundly enlarged view of the world. What about a great business idea? In the event of a divorce, could you easily support you and your kids, half of the time, without the need to be financially supported by a romantic partner? No? Why not? Some of you are still not sure that what I am saying matters or even should matter to your present-day life.

But it does.

Your girls and boys are watching you and they generally struggle along the same path of your leadership example.

A stronger female can bring essential balance to a relationship's circumstances and chemistry. I challenge you to renegotiate your values. Permit reality. A new and exciting world is within reach. Consider that when you feel depressed, you are often spending far too much time coveting what someone else probably taught you to "need" or expect. So you sit in dark places thinking about the way things were supposed to be.

I ask: *"What about the way things are?"*

Is reality not to be admitted? Discovered?

When you start to accept the way things really *are*, you find a tool for getting what you want: creative ability and inspiration. Your resources dislodge when fantasy wish-lists are discarded. You start *learning reality*, which adds the potential for remarkable improvement in your life's quality.

If you intelligently strive to be healthy and mentally sound, the learning process will never end for you. You will constantly shape the world and allow yourself to be shaped by her. I can admit that my values have often shifted back and forth before finally storming forward on the most accurate paths of truth. Carl Rogers (1961) is known for his saying, "The facts are friendly," and indeed they are friendly if you are romantically engaged *with reality*.

MATURING PARENTS AND A CHILD'S BEST INTEREST

The bottom line is that I want moms and dads to be afforded solid opportunities to operate in balanced synergy, presenting children with an effective parenting solution and operating as participants in a supportive family, even if a divorced family. Furthermore, **ideally**, I don't mind if a mom or dad wants to stay home and take care of kids, so long as the stay-at-home parent has a college degree or vocational training prior to doing so. In matters of custody legislation, while perhaps well intended, legal traditions that favor a sole physical custodian can result in severe damage to children and also to the *alienated* parent. The parent who stays home has traditionally been female. She conveniently becomes the normal choice for taking full physical responsibility of the kids, perpetuating our social problem.

I am afraid that nobody is "winning" custody cases right now. Certainly, the adult members of divorced families are not being required to experience genuine mutual accountability. Responsibly coparenting kids together as a dad and mom (even if divorced or never married) cultivates adult maturity, and eventually, confidence in <u>each</u> parent. Such a situation is **exactly what kids need**.

A mature mother and a mature father do not individually result in a mature parenting *experience* for kids. It takes a collective parenting team of both parents *working together* and learning from mistakes. In fact, with both parents being treated as 100% equal in the eyes of family courts, a tenaciously appropriate level of accountability can elevate the parenting team's previously assumed thresholds. That, my friend, is not a perfect process, now is it? You need a big screen to see it, and most people work off of very limited perspectives. Just because the beauty of maturity is not obvious on a daily basis, does not make it any less miraculous in hindsight.

Maturing parents are in the best interest of children and often, during the initial stages of a divorce, neither parent is actually mature individually or cohesively as a parental team. As already mentioned, our outdated legislation tends to feed that problem by getting in the middle of family progress.

On the other hand, if extended the legal mandate to present *our own* parenting plan, we have an opportunity to manage our families by taking the road less traveled. In fact, unique opportunities to shock the attorneys and judge who preside over our divorce case are perfectly fine if the best interest of our children is the driving priority.

As parents, we *are* allowed to present our case as unique-as anomalies of a broken society. We *are* allowed to manage ourselves and our divorced family with common sense. When we walk into a courtroom, hopefully after much deliberation and banter with the other parent, we *are* often allowed to present a better plan than our attorney or judge had in mind; a plan that actually looks out for the best interests of our entire divorced family.

This type of innovation I speak of is, in many states, perfectly legal, and from my own experience, very effective. I am talking about *true* shared parenting resulting in a functional family for children to love and be loved.

Shared parenting is the natural way. Mom presents the biological egg, Dad the sperm, and the rest is a lifetime of new opportunities involving a family whether marriage or divorce are ever involved. As a society, we cannot help the permanency of parenting roles or the often unplanned circumstances that lead to another human's conception. However, if we really love children and the future adults they become, we must work within ambiguity.

I believe that courts should mandate that <u>both</u> parents change everything in their world to accommodate American childhood with 50/50 physical parental responsibilities. The final negotiated details may be different for every family, of course, since every situation is different, including personalities, natural immaturities, and socioeconomic factors.

The role of fulltime single mom is **not acceptable** when a dad exists. As long as parents work out realistic details, it is not the court's business to modify anything unless the plan is obviously lacking some-how. As already mentioned, divorce mediation can be made mandatory for parents who cannot seem to work out a realistic plan.

Now, if the standard presumption for every family court was 50/50 physical and legal responsibility for both parents, then in a situation where one of the parents proved totally disinterested, the court system would then need to naturally step in with a child support mandate.

For those of you stuck on stupid, a parent's role is not to provide child support. When appropriate, temporary <u>ALIMONEY</u> makes a lot more sense as a means to temporarily balance budgets between parents. After the dust settles, a mom should be expected to support herself without a male to subsidize her existence. Child support is a ridiculous notion when you consider that dads should be responsible to take care of children just as moms do, with the exact same investment. Dad's role <u>is</u>

and *should be* treated the same as Mom's role when a divorce occurs: to take care of the kids; and that is a very *involved* role.

Another revolutionary thought. During a divorce or any basic custody hearing, both parents should be obligated within a reasonable timeframe to take physical residence in or near the current school district of the children. A **realistic** divorced parenting plan is always the goal and it is not realistic to attempt shared parenting when parents are torn between school districts. Following the divorce, all relocations must occur **as a family** or not at all.

POLITICIANS

We have a moral obligation as moms and dads to demand the presentation of updated legislation. What are the demands?

1) Presumed 50/50 *Shared Physical Custody Plans*
2) Zero Tolerance for Relocating Children from a Parent
3) Aggressive Removal of Permanent Child Support *During* 50/50 Shared Parenting Situations
4) Simplification of Custody Changes

Did you notice that *number three* makes a lot of sense? Many parents might inevitably use child support as a temporary or permanent source of income, when it is not inherently designed to support an adult. It is supposed to support children. When alimony is actually appropriate, it is in a mom or dad's best interest to be sure that temporary alimony payments are differentiated. If alimony is actually appropriate, it should be paid regardless of how the parenting plan evolves. I am personally still paying alimony today and it has nothing to do with my shared parenting agreement. It would not be in the best interest of children to potentially compromise a visitation arrangement because of money corruption.

Child support should be assumed as *temporary*, requiring the other parent to assume equal childcare responsibilities before elimination. In any case, as mentioned in number four, the laws should be greatly simplified to allow inexpensive changes in custody without requiring a legal battle. In fact, simplification should involve the submission of a basic court document and then the completion of a structured assessment from a private, licensed family professional. Changes in custody should be simple and affordable for any parent showing an active interest. The custody games must stop. The answers are right in front of us.

If you read this book and agree with what I have to say or if you are already aware of the need for *true* shared parenting, then starting today, make demands for legislative changes. Send out a letter to your state representatives. If you send me a copy of the letter(s) and the stamped envelope(s), I will send you the next *digital edition* of this book at no cost. I might even publish your letters as a form of accountability, ensuring that your state representatives listen (see Appendix J for details). Readers? Visit your post office and get your letters sent.

If you are a state representative, I think you are about to receive some letters that ought to be taken seriously. A highly circulated publication of the letters with an accompanying report of your state's legislative results will explain to your voters what you are really in office to achieve. Is it a paycheck? A challenge? Well, here comes the challenge of your career: Ignore the readers of this book. Many of them, perhaps more than 50% of your constituents, have been harmed by the legislation in your state. I am sure the readers from your state didn't even know your name until today, but now they know your name.

The 2007 State of Georgia legislative session produced some very progressive changes that help me sleep a little more comfortably as a responsible dad. Each day, I risk the fragile psychology of my children under this state's jurisdiction. But there is more work to do, even in Georgia. If any readers know of a better way to modify the family court custody assumptions, please notify me. I will listen.

PARENTS

Parents, have I lost your interest due to the responsibility and discomfort that you feel with what I have suggested so far? I understand. Life is tough if we are to do the *most right* things for our next generation. As an author, I will be open to your criticism. Perhaps we can work together on a win-win for the majority of the audience this book will attract.

Mom-reader and Dad-reader, I probably do not personally know you, but realize that my heart is large for you. I want you to feel pride about your better decisions in life…and sometimes the tougher choices include fewer pats on the back. Some choices are selfish for reasons of a higher calling. I am calling you now: Read the remaining chapters, send letters to your legislators, and make shared parenting your first option.

My Story

You may need to read the remainder of this book more than once. You will know you actually "get it" when something strange happens. Either a highly emotional or intellectual moment may occur as all the lights come on and the variables finally fit together for the first time. For this to happen, you might even need to share this book with the person you are divorcing.

When you feel your chest relax about this particular area of your divorce, you will be able to focus on other important areas. If you catch the reality of your situation prior to finalizing things, your entire divorced family could be 100 times happier than it would have been. You won't be able to see how much happier the family is at first. It's hard to know how happy you are that you have a job until you lose it. Families can be the same way. It's hard to see how much happier your divorced family is five years from now unless you botch that divorce agreement. If the agreement is unfair, you, your kids and the other parent will have to live in hell for a very long time. Eventually, I hope you will look back and consider this book as an incredible personal tool, producing some of the most intense *late-breaking* moral and mental leadership growth.

Divorce can sometimes feel like a dangerous game of shortcuts, manipulation and even fear. Your kids would like it if it wasn't at all like this. It doesn't have to be.

So read this carefully and as often as you need. You have a piece of my heart and soul. It's real. Understand that the stakes are much higher than you might have been thinking; and the truth, not as simple.

Remembering my Parent's Divorce

An interesting thing happened to me several years ago. As a young man in my late twenties, I finally cried over how excruciatingly painful my parents' divorce was for me. The divorce happened when I was six. Within a couple years, my mom decided to fall in love with a man who lived several hours away from my father. Let me re-phrase that from an adult's perspective. My mom decided *to relocate* us kids to live with her new man. Though I love my stepfather dearly, this decision placed a considerable amount of distance between us kids and our biological father.

You can decide if I am right to say this or not, but a certain part of me now believes my mom's decision was inexcusable. She did not protect her boys or my father from the years of pain that still haunt us, even today. It was her responsibility to make moral choices, not us kids, and if you think that a divorcing parent is not morally obligated to protect the parental bonds of the other parent, I suggest you seek some intense therapy to figure out why you feel that way. I don't care if my mom felt that my dad was a psychotic redneck during the breakup. The truth is, with some clear boundaries, things could have eventually worked out fine. My dad was not a perfect man; my mom wasn't a perfect woman. But I needed <u>both</u> of my parents and Mom clearly stole that away from her sons. Why? To be with a new husband who would provide more stability and sophistication than my piece-of-shit father ever could. Funny thing about that piece of shit, he sure did spend a lot of time with his boys before the divorce, which is more than I can even say for myself prior to my own divorce.

My dad was gone.

Essentially, without exaggerating this, the father-son bonds were systematically destroyed by a rape. That *everyday* feeling of physical contact that my brother and I shared with our father was irrevocably lost. And I love my mom for choosing Larry, and I can't work past the relocation either. She introduced me to a great man with a new perspective. I would never have understood any of this without the inclusion of Larry in my life; but the cost was unbearable to my fragile little spirit. I broke inside and I still hurt, even in my thirties.

I want my dad back in the critical years when I really needed him.

I did need my stepfather Larry. My mom was perfectly right to leave my real father. AMEN to that divorce. She went out and selected someone better suited for her and Larry brought balance to her boys, so she knew exactly what she was doing. I just needed both dads. Does that make sense?

As an adult, the first sign of latent grief surfaced when my kid's mom, Shauna, reviewed and commented on my "Me-Book" from the seventh grade. The little book had just been dusted off after I happened upon it in an old cardboard box. Her comments shocked me as she pointed out how dark that book was.

"Were you depressed when you were a kid?"

The years had put so much distance between my adult life and my world as a child that I had forgotten what it was like. With the rediscovery of the dusty old book, I pushed myself to enter into emotional reflection about that time period. As I began pulling up the repressed feelings of my growing up experience, an unexpected "integration" of facts hit me.

And I began to sob uncontrollably.

The court system and my own mom treated my biological father as a lesser parent, and this seemed to cut at the very heart of him. He was powerless to stop the social system that yanked our lives apart. I watched a passionate dad be brought to his knees. There was no mercy.

What was he to do? Kidnap us? I might have appreciated that kind of effort from him, since the situation's absolute horror was clear to everyone in my family except my mom and that ridiculous excuse for a court. Thanks for nothing California!

Maybe the divorce had taken her out of her right mind. Maybe she felt that she had married too young and that she needed to get some real distance between her and that lousy marriage with my father. Regardless, my own needs were shoved to the side as irrelevant, and I began entertaining fantasies of a powerful force coming in to save me from losing my dad. Why wasn't Dad strong enough to change the inertia of events?

Please Dad.

Surely you can do something about this.

Help us not lose each other.

PLEASE Dad.

Please? Don't you love us anymore?

WHAT TYPICAL DIVORCE DOES TO DADS

It's astounding to me that people wonder how dads can act like lesser people sometimes during and after a divorce. It's because we are treated like members of a lesser class, a hindrance to the parenting equation. We are disrespected as humans and it makes me sob right now to remember the panic in my life when the marriage with Shauna was no longer healthy enough for us to justify. The thought of my kids not having *Dad* as a real part in their **daily lives** was emotionally crushing to me. As if divorce alone isn't hard enough.

But the courts do not sympathize with men. We are not supposed to be emotionally intelligent. We are either supposed to be "selfish assholes," or we are to show inhuman amounts of "maturity" with regard to the rape that systematically happens to us. We are not supposed to act like we are losing everything that made our lives whole, especially the part involving our role as a *father*.

I wonder about *maturity* sometimes.

Maybe in divorce, fathers act like we are losing everything because we typically do lose everything. Not only are we personally violated, but that pain is then amplified by knowing we will have to sit and watch as our own kids slowly realize their own sharp and painful violation. Our natural responses of hostility and protectiveness are treated as another reason why men shouldn't have custody of their kids.

"They must lack the maturity."

Oh really?

Let's put moms in the child custody position that dads have suffered in for generations- and I mean the EXACT position. Let's see how rational moms are and how well they can emotionally suck it up. No. That doesn't solve anything either, but maybe the rhetoric will help moms to understand where some of the strange and "immature" defensiveness can originate during a divorce.

I am a dad. I wouldn't say any of this if it weren't exactly what typically happens, and really, you already know these things. It is almost an unspoken rule: Stay married, men, or lose everything. The passionate romance in marriages will probably not improve with the advice women are reading in Cosmo; not when men know a gun is constantly being held against their hearts. Once kids are born, it seems to me that such an acute awareness would distract men, destroying the potential for stronger romantic feelings. Men can't help but to focus on the trap they walked headlong into.

Never saw it coming.

Are you aware of what we teach dads?

Go ahead and get close to your kids so that you can have your heart ripped out of you and your wallet exploited when the divorce attorney comes knocking.

Mom not only takes those kids and that money, but then she likely will also remarry, adding another source of income. The 100% provable result is that Mom ends up more capable of providing a totally unfair lifestyle for herself, her new husband, and the children. This situation has got to stop and I mean **now**. It has gone on long enough, and there are readily available alternatives to this.

MY OWN DIVORCE

I am grateful that <u>my</u> kids' mom loved us all enough to risk her "good mommy" social identity by making the best choices for each member of our little family. There was nothing easy about those choices, and the male superior court judge made her feel like a bad mom for loving her family and her future coparenting partner with an honesty that makes others moms quiver at their foundations. There are some people who probably think, *"Well, she obviously was exploited by a manipulating smooth talking ex-husband. She should have taken everyone's advice and simply stopped acknowledging him altogether, and then she would have that man's testicles in a vice right now where they should be."*

Is that what you're thinking?

Do you know what Shauna did? What the right thing was in our situation? She included in the decree that I be identified as the full-custodial parent with a 50/50 visitation schedule.

I am starting to sob again as I write this.

I can't help it.

Not only did I get the natural 50/50 visitation arrangement, but she also handed me the ***outrageous gun*** that the courts typically hand to a mom. I immediately unloaded that gun and set it aside forever. It is not ethical, but outright immoral for one parent to hold functional power over another parent's ability to be a mom or dad. I mean, it's scary when you really think about it.

Regardless of her rationale for making that choice, I have had nothing but respect for Shauna since that day in court and my awe grows more each year as we coparent together. You want to talk about sexy?

You want to talk about brave? Meet a mom who stands up for herself and her divorced family in ambiguous circumstances. Meet my kid's mom.

The difficult thing was that I was not a fully developed dad yet, much like most dads unfortunately, so it truly was an act of faith on her part as a mom. After all, she was the one who had spent so much time with the kids at home in the most difficult years. Now that I actually understand what she was going through firsthand, I call those early years of childrearing "the dark years". You know, the years where the kids get ear infections and wake up screaming in the night. The expensive diaper bills, kids who can't yet articulate why they are screaming at the top of their lungs due to some painful gas or bowel movement. Those are the years when parents lose some sanity, probably forever. It is why I have so much respect for those who have made it to the other side, no matter what their personal issues are. And let's be honest here, all parents have some issues, especially younger couples who foolishly or accidently procreate too early.

Getting back to my legal divorce, it never should have been Shauna's sole responsibility to make decisions about my equal rights as a father. She perceived, as all moms should have in that situation, that an impossible choice had to be made. She had to stand up in a room full of people and say, *"Yes, your honor, I know what I am doing. Clay should be the full-custodial parent."* Meanwhile, the whole time she believed that she could also provide quality care for her babies. The sole public pressure on a divorcing young mom is sickening. Take all of the child-care responsibilities or you are not a good mom. Right?

WHAT SHOULD BE HAPPENING: REAL MEDIATORS STAND UP!

Perhaps the reason we feel we need divorce attorneys is because moms are being forced into difficult choices that shouldn't normally be available. The person a mom *should be* talking to is the kids' father, negotiating a working arrangement of shared parenting variables.

It is unnecessary to suggest that one parent is more qualified than the other to make decisions about a child's life. <u>Both</u> parents naturally should have equal input, and <u>both</u> **can** use diplomatic tools, married or divorced. It's that simple. Mom and Dad are naturally half-custodial parents creating a full-custodial solution for kids. The State of Georgia did not permit two custodial parents and that is completely unacceptable.

You say, *"You just don't understand the person I am divorcing. It is impossible to talk to him/her."*

My reply, *"Sounds like a damn good reason to divorce someone."*

Today, after years of working out the interpersonal kinks, I share a rock-solid 50/50 visitation arrangement with Shauna. As parents, we work together on all aspects of parenting and we are routinely discussing the developing young man and the two young women we are raising. As a child of divorce however, I wasn't afforded opportunities to see my parents working together like this.

Perhaps in your situation, you feel that the skills are not available between you and the other parent to successfully coparent. There is an inexpensive solution for difficult situations: a practical, objective, experienced *coparenting mediator*.

I personally offer this service for divorcing couples using telephone conference calls or simple webcams. The hassle of using a mediator is worth it to your entire family. Not only do you get quicker and smoother fixes to the most emotionally taxing issues, but after using a solid mediator a few times, you eventually learn to figure out most problems together, without assistance. In the end, you end up having a safety net waiting if an emergency occurs.

I know that the idea might sound less traditional and strange to consider. The alternative is to **not** use a comfortable, experienced and objective referee. Either way, you must keep in mind that high-velocity arguing should NEVER be in front of your kids-NEVER, EVER, EVER.

Shauna and I got along "so-so" when we would solve problems as a married couple. We were both very unhealthy and perhaps I was worse. Not all divorcing couples start ahead like this. Some can hardly be in the same room with the other parent. So to take the pressure off of both of you, get a solid coparenting mediator until you don't need one anymore.

In your official divorce agreement's parenting plan, I would include the use of coparenting mediation when making difficult decisions *if necessary*. Simply agree together that if you can't resolve an issue, you will share the expense of using a mediator. The cost can be around $50 an hour. That's a small price to pay for keeping things smooth.

Using a mediator is proactive, reasonable, and very smart.

SPECIAL NOTE ON ABUSIVE SITUATIONS

If a mom or dad attempt to intimidate the other parent with threats *to anyone's* <u>safety</u> at any time, I feel like ALL evidence should be permitted as legal grounds for the <u>temporary</u> revoking of the abuser's parenting visitation. Dads and moms, if you cannot refrain from verbal abuse, you will have a seriously expensive road ahead of you. Nobody is going to sympathize with any type of threatening behavior. It's like joking about having a bomb with you while at the airport. People will take your threats seriously **because they have to**. If you have been acting like an idiot in the past, or felt like saying something stupid, remove that option <u>now</u>. Be smart.

There should be zero tolerance for physical or verbal abuse. We need strict enforcement of *high-accountability* parenting training for physical and verbal abusers.

People have to learn that primitive manipulation doesn't help anything *in the long run*. It hurts all parties involved, especially children. We can all try getting what we want, the *right* way, when we know how to use the right tools. Once we start using the right tools and continue to reject the harmful tools, *long run* rewards will finally catch up to us.

Right?

It is a matter of learning. For those who refuse to learn, an eventual loss of freedom will take over. A series of missed opportunities for the entire family is at risk.

For those of you who are squirming right now, know that it does get better if you listen to what I have said in this section. When you realize that there are issues with understanding the person you had kids with, chalk it up to irreconcilable differences. Those differences may have led to the divorce, but they don't have to ruin your kids' childhood or your parenting experience.

BACK TO MY PARENTS

I remember growing up with my mom and dad trying to coparent over the phone. These phone conversations would often end abruptly with my dad calling my mom a bitch and hanging up. Looking back, from his perspective, I think he might have been right in his overall personal assessment. Knowing what I know as a divorced adult, when really considering the overall situation our divorced family was in, from his limited perspective, my mom behaved far worse than a spoiled-rotten bitch could have. My dad should not have been calling her names. Name calling is a form of verbal abuse so my biological father is a prime example of a parent who lacked education/training. He needed a realistic parenting and coparenting class.

By now, you understand that I am educated and very respectful of customary language practices, so naturally if I had been in his exact mental frame of mind, I myself would have called her a *fuckin' bitch*.

But that's just me.

Admittedly, my mom was perfectly within her legal rights. Give her a brownie and a USA patch for taking full advantage of her role as a legally compliant mom. Did her **moral compliance** matter at all? I really hope my mom was able to "find herself" in the new marriage because the rest of us quickly lost ourselves.

We were just kids. My dad was a seriously uneducated redneck. He didn't have any awareness of concepts like shared parenting or parenting education. In fact, he can't even read. There was little to work with for either parent.

Nausea.

My mom made the best decision for her life and that is commendable. My dad was financially poor, and perhaps initially unaware of how difficult he and his kids would accept my mother's relocation. In the end, he couldn't afford to drive eight hours to see us every other weekend, and it would have ruined much of everyone's quality of life if he had tried. The hardship involved was unrealistic for the parenting equation. It was morally lacking and ultimately, tragic for everyone.

At the time, my brother and I only wanted to keep the peace and we didn't want to see *either* of our parents hurting. My stepfather? He would say the phrase: "Kids belong with their mother." Thankfully, **my kid's mom** made a different conclusion when she considered who <u>our</u> babies belong with. Shauna has been a *stand-up* mom throughout our entire divorced parenting situation. We have made it work as a parenting team, and it hasn't been easy.

I am also thankful that Shauna, *however uncomfortably,* assumed personal responsibility for providing her own fiscal success. She skipped child support and settled for a *very appropriate* alimony scenario. That is because I do my part. I provide a <u>quality</u> home for the kids to live, half of the time.

I use the word "ideal" quite often in this publication. Sometimes I frown on idealism and sometimes I think it should be admitted that an ideal circumstance actually exists, even when we accidently or intentionally deviate from ideal circumstances. In an ideal world, alimony might not be necessary at all. However, the fact is that Shauna did not have the same earning potential as I did at the time of the divorce, simply because she had not been working on a professional career while the children were younger. This did not make Shauna less capable of professional employment, simply less ready. This is exactly why alimony was appropriate for her financial budget. The alimony was designed to be temporary and therefore, a scheduled departure from her ex's financial support would occur once the playing field naturally leveled.

While many parents "help" their daughters by pointing them to a man's dutiful financial support, I won't be cultivating inappropriate *male dependence* in my daughters. Today, Shauna's occupational independence reinforces the fact to my kids that a woman can take care of herself, without a man. Shauna's father has become very interested in her *professional* success, and that is what I hope to experience with my daughters as well.

KNOWING THYSELF KEEPS IT HEALTHY

I would prefer that my daughters not think that they will find themselves in a marriage. That is simply a repulsive thought as it would sabotage each daughter's *individual* self-worth. In fact, it would set each daughter up to stay in unhealthy relationships, desperately clinging to some sense of wholeness. With the right support, hopefully Kayla and Angela will not *need* a man to take care of them or to make them feel special. They already are special for what they are capable of doing and who they are capable of becoming. The only reason why either daughter should enter into a relationship is to **share** what they have with another gifted person. Romantic relationships are truly optional and <u>always</u> subject to change. My apologies to the hopeless romantics, but sometimes relationships become too sick; even impossible.

It is not life and death if a relationship fails. In all fairness, the only thing that ever dies is an agreement to be together *romantically*. For kids, even a divorced family stays alive when parents work out a shared visitation schedule. It is perfectly okay for parents to clearly communicate that the romantic involvement between Mom and Dad is over. The love for the children involved, including active involvement from both parents, is clearly not over.

We are all special and we <u>can</u> always *continue to love* those we have been romantic with, but folks, life and personal happiness DO NOT depend on a fucking relationship. Get it! Feel it. Smell it. **KNOW IT.**

BREAKING UP AND FEELING PSYCHO

You are capable of breaking up with someone, eventually dating someone else, and hopefully selecting a person who is better qualified or more compatible with you.

Stop acting pathetic and manipulative. Let your ex be a separate human with REAL HUMAN FREEDOM to do what he/she wants with life. Do you think another human is a piece of your property just because you both participated in a high-pressure cultural ceremony? How sick is that? A soul cannot be owned. Is your ex a pet of yours or something? You want to train another person? You want to **make** someone want you? Feelings like this indicate that you didn't actually know how to the love the other person. That awareness should disturb you if you still want the other person to stay. Of course it could just be a control issue. *"Hey I wasn't done with you yet. You can't leave until I say you can."*

Hopefully, once you have had time to adjust to reality again, the emotional bankruptcy will pass, as it can, and you will feel okay to be out of the relationship, especially if you often wanted out or should have wanted out. Following any separation, empty feelings can surface, really confusing feelings. They are normal and not a reason to think anything, other than that the incompatible romantic relationship has actually ended.

No kidding, right?

Instead of spending your time living life through the other person, which is sick, maybe you should learn how much <u>you</u> have already changed; and understand that life has many new options that will feel *most perfect* once you have had time to get your emotions, brain, and financial situation stabilized again. ALL feelings of insanity will pass; even the silly insane feelings about **forcing** your soon-to-be-ex into listening to you about whatever it is you feel like they need to hear. Get your priorities straight. Get healthy. You might be amazed at how many people listen when you have the right motives.

This year a father in Washington State killed his five children before taking his own life. The father did this as retaliation for his wife's decision to leave the marriage for another man. The marriage had included noteworthy fighting, at times even requiring the involvement of social workers. The end result was a house full of dead children, a dead dad, and a mom waiting...to wake up from an impossible nightmare.

You really need to get your thinking cap on. I have felt the pain and frustration of an unwanted breakup. I have been cheated on. I have cheated. At times like these, we can embarrass ourselves by saying or doing things that are out of character. In the end though, life goes on and I can finally say that I love my life right now, more than when I was married. Had I become too engrossed in the insane feelings of the breakup, I could have made decisions that might have been unrecoverable.

Keep your goals clear, especially when you know something has upset you emotionally. The feelings will pass and the goals will probably still remain. Do not keep yourself from your own goals. Psycho feelings are hardly worth the trouble they are capable of causing.

Refreshing surprises probably await you within a few years outside of a divorce. Shauna and I have come a long way over the last few years. You will too. Many of us would prefer to avoid pain and we also tend to initially respond with fear to potential changes in our lifestyle. But an *unwanted* divorce is sometimes the clearest indication that we have a lot more learning to do about life and love and our marriage was probably not helping us learn it.

My point is that people who are taught to find identity in a person or marriage will probably never find themselves. Yet how many men and women actually feel special, whole and complete without a lover to depend on like a leach? I am not talking about companionship and sharing. I am talking about the idea that life has no meaning at all and that the whole of self-esteem and happiness must depend on *someone else* to give you a thumbs up or to be your lifetime scapegoat.

Look, emotional and physical abuse is not on the menu for my intelligent daughters *or* my son.

I actually know men and women alike who demand that their current lover forsake all of his or her friends of the opposite sex before a romantic relationship can be considered "satisfying." Really, these individuals who make such demands are not qualified to be dating so seriously. A stronger partner would be needed to immediately correct that type of backwards thinking.

Why would I suggest that it's "unhealthy" for someone to forsake their opposite-sex friends? It's because those friends are there for a reason. The individual demanding that friends be discarded is seeking a safe relationship. It is my opinion that the "perfectly safe" relationship is a total illusion and probably, not very healthy. My daughters can love a man and be loved without making the relationship sick in order to feel safe. Unhealthy insecurities are most easily dealt with through communication and a more serious analysis of the relationship's merit. Maybe it isn't a good enough fit to trust in?

What's your approach to a romantic partner having "dangerous" friends? Your answer will probably not surprise me at all- especially if you have ever been "cheated" on. I think insecurities can be useful. They challenge the entire premise of the relationship's seriousness. If *someone else* **is** actually better somehow, then why be together at all? Or maybe two people shouldn't be treating the relationship like its secure when it isn't. Maybe I am stupid, but I thought relationships are based on solid facts. Either you are taking your time while dating someone to determine the relationship's potential or you already know the facts. If you already know the facts about how great the relationship is, what's to be insecure about? I can't think of a damn thing myself.

I think people are insecure because they feel like controlling the person they love. Why not just get a job that allows you to get that "controlling" urge out of our system before getting home? That would make more sense.

MY STEPFAMILY

Speaking of situations that improve or reduce opportunities to cultivate self-esteem, my stepsister and stepbrother were also eventually relocated. They moved out of state with their mother and thus, away from their dad and their second home. For years I wonder if Jennifer blamed her dad for letting it happen.

Did he really not love her?

Wasn't he even interested in her life?

Did he feel **any** *emotional connection towards her?*

You can't oversimplify that situation. Larry had a moral right to shared parenting, but minimal legal rights and even less social backing. In respect to my stepfather's mode of operation, I think he knew that allowing emotions inside of a legal situation was to be foolishly vulnerable. Everything is business in the end and everything will be fine in the end. While this often might be true of our intellectual strategy, emotional awareness paints a much fuller world that might not be okay *at all*. Emotional sensitivity in a legal world is suicide for most critical thinkers, especially dads who become separated from their kids' daily lives. Only so many times can a smart individual be burned before pulling back and calling it what it is- an emotional killing field that needs to be respected, rather than allowed deep inside.

There was indeed a maturing process for Larry to experience. Perhaps his daughter and son could have helped him through that processes over the years, and yet the parental bond was broken when it really counted.

His kids should have NEVER been relocated. I witnessed his loss, even though he allowed the relocation to occur. Don't think this sort of thing doesn't impact the human development and self-esteem of adults and children alike. Relocations do have a substantial negative impact on parenting and this type of damage is preventable through custody legislation reform. When both parents feel like legitimate parents, the likelihood of relocations will be reduced significantly due to the emotional connections that naturally develop.

The visitation arrangement between Larry and his ex ended up **cruel** to everyone. Yet it was beyond Jennifer and Sean's control, just as it was out of their dad's reasonable control and apparently out of their mom's *reasoning* control. If I remember correctly, Jennifer's mom even attempted to have Larry's parental rights discarded and replaced by an adoption from her new husband; change of last names included!

What is that?

Had Larry's ex not also called his fatherhood a total loss? Whose fault was this, if anyone's? What causes this type of disaster? I think I know what set off the chain of events and I think the adults involved know too. Somehow the personal issues from those young divorcing parents got morally out of control, even destructive.

If he can't be a dad with me, he must not be a dad at all.
PRIDE!!!
HURT!!!
JEALOUSY!!!
And the kids are the ones that suffer.

New lives get started and while the adults might look back later and see how it all happened, it's far too late to recover the lost years and the trauma that occurred as a result.

My stepfather had to try sleeping every night knowing that the mom talking to his kids and taking care of their daily lives wanted *his remaining rights legally removed!* And <u>this</u> was the quality of coparenting that everyone suffered with. Jennifer and Sean's mother lost the "adoption" battle. I am sure that somehow the kids' mom thought it was best to pretend that Dad wasn't really Dad anymore. After all, he wasn't ever around, was he? He had a new family, didn't he? He was trying to be happy with the mess things became, wasn't he?

The legal and social arrangement had stripped Larry of feeling like a respected parent to his kids. He dumped himself further into his job.

*"Now kids, you have a new dad who is here **a lot more**."*

Dads often lose hope of ever feeling like a dad again to *their own* kids following a divorce. Child support machines, and every-other-weekend childcare, that's what our court system has made dads into. Our nation's parenting situation has brutalized dads, kids and moms for years, and meanwhile, you actually bash dads for complaining and finally departing the absurd game of: "Give me your money *bitch* and make sure I have ***my kids*** back by six p.m. on Sunday."

DAD ON THE OFFENSE

You might be thinking that I am attempting to appeal to your sensitivities by using emotionally charged words like "cruel" and "tragic." I might be. But if you are seriously thinking that my situation growing up was *not cruel*, I have something to say to you.

*"Stay away from me and **my** kids. Okay?"*

"We clear on that much?"

You don't think that your kids actually need their dad. The little problem you can't fully grasp is that *you thought* your kids were bad before? *You thought* you had no help with the kids before? You are about to rape *yourself* of anything resembling healthy parenting. Count your self-esteem as toast too, because you know that what you are about to do is morally irreprehensible even if others say it's okay. You are about to sell your soul and you are going to do it thinking you are "taking care of the kids."

Someone who rationalizes my *childhood* visitation arrangement away as being "the best thing" needs to understand how *extremely protective* over <u>my kids</u> I am. Male or female, you threaten my daily father-child relationship with the typical sick sympathy for our culture's wrong expectations about divorced parents, and I will get so upset I will have to throw up on you.

Chunky vomit all over your face.

I have seen enough heartache to break me for the rest of my life. I don't need you helping my kids. I want my kids to have self-esteem. I want self-esteem, and I want my first wife, the mother of my kids to have it too. My kids are aware that every week of their life, Mom and I stand guard, reassuringly protecting their development. I don't need a fucking court to help me with that by suggesting I be an every-other-weekend parent. So get your paws into someone else's life and "help" them as if they are completely incompetent.

Jesus Christ, please save these idiots from hurting my family or anyone else. Baptize them in the name of honesty and intelligent perception beyond their years. May they stop continuing this cycle of social stratification and minority oppression at the expense of my family or someone else's.

Or maybe Jesus isn't going to save anyone from this. Maybe instead, dropping some basic letters in the mail to your lawmakers might save us all on this particular issue. In your own divorce, maybe **you** will need to do the saving.

I want you and your divorced family to have self-esteem. It doesn't happen over night either, since we are all pretty screwed up on any given day. I don't care how much you deny it. The more someone denies they have issues, the more layers of problems I know they are carefully cultivating and are not processing.

As humans, considering all of our mistakes, it sure does help to know that we really have done our best to make morally accurate choices. Such decisions must involve the use of logic **and** emotional honesty as the most important influencers. Other people don't make our choices for us. We own our decisions, or else we are nothing more than sell-outs; and sell-outs are empty shells with no *soul* understanding.

When someone's unhealthy ideas about child custody appear to threaten the reputation or candor of me as a father or Shauna as a mother, when my moral right to half of the parental visitation schedule is reduced by someone, when my ability to work within a fair financial budget **without** paying my ex-wife child support is ignorantly ridiculed, I feel like fighting back to protect five things: Kayla, Andrew, Angela, myself and my coparenting partner- the members of *my* divorced family.

Why am I not a miserably defeated individual who feels disconnected from reality? Why do my kids have an active father raising them with their active mother? Thank my ex-wife, Shauna. She respected me as a dad when nobody else would take a chance. At the time of the divorce, Shauna's dad and my dad both seemed to feel that the kids belonged with their mother and that I might need to have two jobs. Both dads ended up being right about almost all of the other advice they offered. How would such brilliant men be so *wrong* on an issue like *divorced parenting*? May I submit that the damage has already occurred to my parent's generation? The hooks have been set and the fish caught.

Guess what? Not only was I depressed throughout my childhood; not only were my siblings depressed; but I get to see new depressed kids when I visit my kids at school. My eyes start to water. I remember going through that when I was a kid.

What are these moms thinking when they go along with the system? I'll bet these same moms are *so* lacking in parenting support from the kids' father, that the kids now require prescription drugs to treat their mental issues, especially the sons; the daughters come later. Mom and dad should have tried something different with child custody and child support. The whole family needed mercy more than mom needed to feel like she got that money coming in now, and she got the kids.

And she got those antidepressants too.

Oh, and in all of it, these moms blame their ex-husbands for ruining their lives.

No, *he didn't*. There are a lot more moving parts than just an ex-husband. He may act like an asshole towards you, but better choices can still be made during divorce. When better choices are made, the family can frequently avoid cruel power games; games borne of fear, hurt and pride. Dad may not always be a jerk and it will be far too late when these moms finally figure it out. The real problems that might ruin a woman's life are more appropriately identified at the macro level. The way many countries have been handling women socially is the issue, and the solution *begins* with fair reform to custody legislation.

I could pray for divorced moms to demonstrate common sense and get those custody papers fairly reworked. But they won't. Not even Jesus could get their heads out of their child support checks now. The American legal system *should have been* protecting those kids and *should have* protected those moms from assuming parenting responsibilities alone.

Readers, this is the real world of our modern divorce law and it's not working. Your attorney will not save you from it once you have paid the fees and signed the papers. Having said that, I am sure the feminist readers, male or female (people I actually agree with more often than not) want to slam me against a wall right now for being so insensitive to the situation of American moms.

Total hypocrites.

It is a social problem, and I shouldn't get so personal about this. But you know what? You who criticize me right now…when was the last time you did something to fix this problem? When was the last time you wrote your legislators to save these moms from needlessly tossing away their sanity into the pit of single motherhood?

This offensive tirade is to notify you readers of one thing: my natural right to parent my children matters and dads can shape up their act if you actually respect them during a divorce. JUST BE FAIR.

My ability to be there for my divorced family matters to each family member; and even to people who date my kids' mom or me. Cooperation and collaboration go a long way during everyday life and difficult transitions.

My ex-wife and I are mutually supportive of each other's situations. We are in it together with our kids and we don't have to live at the same house or sleep in the same bed to have each other's backs. We also don't have to agree on everything, but we continually try to improve how we negotiate with every parenting disagreement.

AND THAT'S HEALTHY FOLKS.

THE LONG MEMORY OF CHILDREN

For many of you, the real trouble with all this is that kids don't really understand *right now* how to recognize when one parent is actually doing the selfish and morally irreprehensible thing. In fact, I think kids are often told things like, *"No matter how hurt you might feel, it has to be this way."*

No. It doesn't.

It really doesn't have to be this way.

There *are* other realistic options. There *are* fair alternatives when the stakes are this high. There are job changes, lifestyle modifications, patience, mediators, and a variety of other tools to help keep things afloat during and after the divorce. One day, such deep sacrifices will not be necessary, but taking care of kids as you make choices right now will make for a better life later.

I recently read in the news about a mom who beat her kid to death. The entire time her two-year old daughter was pleading for mercy, saying, "I love you Mommy. I love you Mommy." Mom continued with the beating and ended the little girl's life. The reason for the fatal beating was that the *TWO-YEAR OLD* had forgotten her formal ma'am-and-sir manners.

Sometimes parents think a child understands exactly what is happening and why it is happening, but the truth is that a child doesn't. There is a certain responsibility to stand up for doing the right thing, even when it goes against the cultural system or social institutions. I am certain that the violent mom of that news story was somehow taught early on that "sir" and "ma'am" are the *respectful* way for youths to address adults.

As a side note, it always troubles me that anyone would think that respect is not perceptually *earned*, but that's another story we will save for a parenting publication. In all truth though, it really does apply here. Dad and Mom, do you earn respect from each other? You might want to start a new trend with how you treat one another, including the infusion of some patience, or you are in for some terribly rough terrain.

The news report is tragic and yes, completely ironic since that mom didn't actually earn respect.

The ideas presented in this book are not sophisticated at all, are they? The concepts so far are based in real-world experience and in common wisdom. Whatever you were taught growing up, or whatever your friends or family are doing or saying to you right now is irrelevant to your future custody scenario- more so than you might imagine. Even if you think your parents are going to be the ones helping you out the most in your post-divorce situation, do you really want them having that much control in your life again? The other half of your sperm/egg creation might have some serious incentive to change his or her life around to share the childcare responsibilities. You would need to present a shared schedule <u>without</u> child support. In a 50/50 scheduled situation, this is reasonable. Budgets can be balanced with negotiated alimony. Alimony depends on multiple factors. If needed, divorce mediators or attorneys can help clarify how alimony relates to your specific situation. In my situation, Shauna and I were able to figure it out for ourselves as we split assets and reviewed budgets.

To establish lasting success, you will eventually need to work together, make clear plans, and have <u>measurable</u> expectations that can be included in a legal parenting plan.

Taking the advice of your friends, family, or new lover is probably not a sound way to parent *your* kids anyway, not when nearly everyone seems to get the child visitation issue wrong. My mom made that mistake and <u>everybody</u> paid. I also failed to mention that my mom does not appear to be a very happy person to this day. The priorities we establish can really set us up to fail miserably at integrating win-win karma in our future. Do you realize that yet? Perhaps you need to read the statement again in full context. ***Everybody*** paid for her mistake in the end.

What does matter?

What makes sense?

What is honest?

What is fair to the big picture?

The ideas in this book are not challenging for me to acknowledge because I have had some time to really inspect the concepts and then test them in my real life. I was not and still am not any better of a parent than the kids' mom. In fact, if I am honest, nowadays we both tend to bring unique strengths to the table that balance out the parenting team. That means that we both have some rather obvious weaknesses too.

My expectation for the remainder of this book is that you get down from your defensive positions. I know that in the last few pages, I've applied pressure to provoke the mom and dad readers to turn their brains on. That makes it hard to not be defensive, *even if* you really had wanted to test out this book's information.

Moms, I am so sorry I had to do that. But I really have to tell this like it is from my horribly damaged position. If the laws were different we would all *feel like* we were on the same team, and we REALLY are. Either way, please realize that dads will be directly dealt with in a later chapter. So Dads, before you march the White House lawn in angry protests, let's get focused.

We are going to pull up our big-boy underwear or our big-girl panties and allow some radical but still commonsense-ideas to creep into our awareness. We are adults, after all, and there is a lot at stake if bad choices are made. Despite what people have told you about the *resiliency* of children, remember that kids *do* finally grow up, and we *don't* forget the quality of life that your choices bring to or steal from our childhood.

My mom is a great mother and grandmother. She is often extremely protective of us. She sacrificed often and I think she did her very best to make her life work.

But her choices also ruined my childhood and it's gone now.

Not to mention the fact that she allowed my dad's emotional exploitation by doing what people probably told her was "okay."

"He'll get over it."

"You have to think about you now."

"He'll just have to finally grow up."

"This is what divorce is."

Resiliency. What a lame atonement for the excuses we make when we ruin a childhood. You see, we were not just our mom's kids. We were our dad's kids too. That is where the root issue is clear.

Dad is not > Mom

Mom is not > Dad

Dad = Mom

This is not difficult math; even your kids could get the answer. Dads and moms are equally important in the week*day* lives of kids.

Brainwashed Parents or Intuitive Problem Solvers

So, here is our newsflash: kids need both Mom and Dad; not just Mom, and not just Dad. If you think that you are solving anything by calling the other parent a low-life, you are wrong. If you think that you can trust your fellow Americans in the belief that, "Kids should be with their moms," you are seriously brainwashed. I think I read somewhere that the successful rock artist Kurt Cobain honestly believed that at least three-quarters of the American population was semi-retarded. Are you in that larger group? We can fix it if you have been living a follow-the-next-ant lifestyle. That's the point of this book, in fact: To wake you up and to do it with a direct and honest informative perspective- a perspective you have probably needed.

I think it is common sense to recognize that chopping your kids in half physically or psychologically like divorcing couples might do with their property is not really optional. Kids don't like being divided by childish parents who can't seem to notice that the children involved in a divorce have rights of protection too, especially from every-other-weekend parenting.

Seasoned Americans forget that this backwards divorce law is still alive and well, *ruining families more than it's helping*. I realize that I ought to sue the hell out of California and give the proceeds to what's left of my dad.

But you know what? I have a better idea. Maybe I will simply find it therapeutic to know that you are actually still reading this right now. Although, Dad, we both know that you and your kids will probably be dealt a fatal blow by Mom's attorney. Mom, you will wonder why he is being such an asshole just because you end up doing everything the attorney you hired says is "normal" and *the right thing in the long run.* But what are we to do? We just go with the flow, don't we? We read our script and live dead lives and raise more mentally capable but functionally retarded adults, just like we turned out to be.

Or maybe you are tired of living life like that.

CAN YOU BELIEVE THAT?

I mentioned "beliefs" earlier and that word can mean many different things. When I mention beliefs, I am not necessarily referring to religious beliefs, though religion can certainly harm or help us.

I consider our nonreligious, unconscious beliefs, to carry a significant amount of power. While many consider circumstances to be the creator of our life, I submit that *how we respond* to circumstances is more pertinent than the circumstances themselves. Our beliefs drive such responses, and these responses to circumstance are where our soul can experience a unique sensation: freedom. To control our destiny more effectively, we must become mindful of our beliefs.

Get a pen.

WARM-UP EXERCISE
Please answer the following questions.

Fear of spiders is an expression of what someone "believes" about spiders. **True or False**

Not all spiders are going to hurt you. **True or False**

The belief about all spiders being dangerous keeps us safer by leaning on the conservative side when confronted with a spider's presence.
True or False

Our beliefs alter our decisions and choices, even when our beliefs are wrong. **True or False**

PARENTING BELIEFS

We have discussed many moral-value pretzels so far, challenging some beliefs that your culture has been slamming you with all your life. Maybe you even feel that there hasn't been much of a choice in the matter of deciding what you believe. Perhaps you have never cared to think about it.

Using a simple approach, let's start integrating concepts with your real situation. In the area of parenting beliefs, a divorce challenges any parent to stretch and rethink how Mom and Dad have both been handling childrearing responsibilities. Often, dads and moms go through marriages without being clear about who should be doing what. In my own case, while married, my kid's mom would actually ask for more help and I was less than cooperative *at the time*. Be completely honest in answering the following questions. This book is yours to keep and nobody needs to see how you answer.

In the space provided below, briefly discuss what you believe to be true about whom a child should be staying with in the event of a divorce.

_____

_____

_____

_____

_____

_____

_____

In one or two sentences, describe what probably formed your belief. Example: *"My ex-husband is not very nurturing,"* or *"My parents have always said that, so I guess I am just old-fashioned."*

DEFENDING YOUR PARENTING BELIEFS

Now consider the general beliefs you have about child custody. Could you defend these beliefs in court? Wait a minute....you don't have to worry about defending any beliefs in court, because in uncontested situations, the court probably won't care if you have any "evidence" either way. In fact, the court has some beliefs too and those beliefs can be summed up in respecting legal tradition; and then getting through your case to get to the next one. It may not be that simple, but then again, I have personally witnessed it happen. In terms of evidence against your ex, there is dirt to be had on many of us parents, so drop the nit-pick list of "evidence." It's not necessary.

Getting back to your specific situation, I need to reiterate a common theme of this book. Just because a couple breaks up in a divorce does not mean that the family should break up to your child. Your children do not see why the family should dissolve just because the romantic marriage dissolves and the kids are right to naturally feel that way. You should listen to the feelings of your kids before you start twisting things to fit what your attorney or your mommy and daddy say is best. Perhaps a far superior idea would be to instead work with the other parent involved. **Secure** a totally fresh approach to parenting in your situation. There are risks involved, but risks can have substantial winnings too, including a stronger sense of personal moral candor.

As far as your children go, it is actually NEVER a good idea to toss responsibility on your kids during a divorce. They really don't know the half of what a divided family will do to their sense of long-term security. Child psychology is very strange. I watch my own kids bounce around between rebellion and attachment; exaggerated independence and even exaggerated concern. One month there might be indifference to mom, with a preference for dad. The next month is might be indifference to dad with a preference for mom. Has it ever occurred to you that a child's freedom to experience this process is actually normal and needed? To remove either parent might actually remove the necessary (and *hopefully* safe) object of rebellion.

While it is true that involving children in a divorce might later create inappropriate guilt, also consider the danger in tossing the baby out with the bathwater. Developmental needs of your children should be a serious consideration- they are the "babies" and the "bathwater" might include games that involve child manipulation. Adults sometimes use games to compensate for personal insecurities.

No, your kids won't get over it if you neglect their needs while looking out for yourself, as evidenced by my mom's GROSS errors in handling her boys during her divorce and post-divorce family evolution. No matter how my mom might have tried denying it, our family was still a family in the eyes of ALL humans involved. If she chose to move two-hundred miles from my father, the fact remained that we were still a family and every day that her boys woke up in Southern California was another day she poured emotional gasoline on our beds and lit the match. She fucked up horribly and should have moved us BACK TO FRESNO; but she didn't. Everyday I woke up for the rest of my childhood knowing that my life was being dictated by something inhuman, a belief system lacking emotional protection. Each day of my life, the integrity of a little boy's childhood was cut into smaller pieces.

ADVICE OF LEGAL PROFESSIONALS

I don't have an issue with attorneys when it comes to knowing the laws well enough to write a bullet-proof divorce agreement that suits what the family needs. If you get anything out of this book, get what I am about to say next:

You might be surprised by the parenting resources your co-parent might produce if you patiently take time to challenge him or her into some <u>fair</u> and *workable* hypothetical scenarios.

Remember, those hypothetical scenarios can have legal teeth when a judge signs the divorce decree. You have plenty of room for honesty and for consideration of yourself and the other parent during the planning process, which might include brainstorming. Personally, I feel that you must consider the other parent involved. Get him or her off the defensive (if possible), and discuss all variables and all possibilities to see where each variable might fit in ways that are fair. Then for several days, take time to consider what is talked about; continue the discussion with your coparenting partner without allowing romantic history in the conversation. Prior to making any important conclusions or decisions, DO NOT involve "concerned" (nosey, negative, or bored) outsiders unless it's an experienced divorce mediator. Most people (including parents, siblings, and friends) should not be allowed to manipulate your decisions since they have *their own* lives to live. Just remember that it's *your divorced family* and <u>**your**</u> **family's quality of life** will not be experienced by anyone else on a daily basis while your kids are growing up. Who will live it? The *members* of your divorced family including kids, Mom and Dad. Once you have determined what you want, you should then direct the individual creating your divorce agreement, and/or a legal professional to make sure that you have all the details covered. I have included a visitation schedule from an actual divorce agreement in Appendix B.

You two started the family, and you two can find a way to get it healthy again. That process is so much easier when you are divorcing rather than continuing to expect the other romantically incompetent party to satisfy your insatiable marital needs. Right? The problems you have with the other party are already known and can be great fuel to **keep negotiating** the divorce *intelligently*.

Attorneys and judges are not the true enemies, though they have often assumed that role due to the weaklings most folks are when it comes to doing the **fair** thing. Why should lawyers put themselves in a situation of liability if something actually goes wrong later? For an attorney, her or his role is inherently to defend herself/himself by staying in the protection of a legal advisory role, explaining your full legal abilities, and informing you of the "general" way people manage their decisions around the law.

What I am suggesting is that **you** are the one who is supposed to figure out how you want to manage your visitation situation and all divorce terms, not a damn attorney who might have no concept of what *effective discussion* with the other parent might accomplish. My understanding of a legal expert's general usefulness is to properly dot the i's and cross the t's of your negotiated, enforceable, and agreeable divorce terms.

You function differently than an attorney does because you will actually be living out the divorce terms *for years;* that attorney will be long gone. You know who will be staring at you? The other parent will be there. Your divorce decisions must be based on available resources, which I suggest, might include a more hopeful understanding of all factors that encourage new energy from the other parent.

Muster the fortitude to take fresh approaches when negotiating the terms of your divorce. Follow my advice here, and your kids will have a much better opportunity to thank you later when they are grown up and are parenting your grandkids. Mom, give your *kids' dad* a copy of this book or give it to someone he will listen to. Dads, do the same thing.

Fear of what the other parent's attorney *might be* scheming is normal in divorce negotiations. It is a common problem that can paralyze a divorcing couple from working out win-wins. Fear can also **fuel** the legal industry making attorneys feel more arrogant as your "legal super-heroes."

Gag me.

Just remember that you don't want a contested divorce, and that your signature of total approval will be needed to really accomplish anything in an uncontested circumstance. So calm down and see this for what it is. You don't sign it, it's not happening. As I like to frequently say, back your finger slowly away from the trigger (or pen) before you hurt yourself or someone else as a result of a fear reflex.

And if your *Super Attorney* needs it, put one of your kid's stinky socks in his or her mouth.

You have more power to negotiate win-win terms with the other parent actively working *with you* than you ever will by taking an intimidating legal position. Such legal positioning often just gums you up from learning and getting a truly fair result. Think about it.

Here is another question.

You live in a country still dominated mostly by white men of power, while women are statistically behind the curve when it comes to credibility and the ability to acquire higher-level jobs at competitive pay?
True or False

YOUR BELIEFS ABOUT GENDER

If you were silly and answered "false," I would like you to immediately go online and look up the board of directors of <u>any</u> major soft drink company or retailer. I also would like you to look at the <u>entire</u> history of US presidents. If you believe that the powerful forces in your country are fans of women being treated as equally intelligent, equally resourceful and equally powerful, you are dead wrong.

I wonder why that is?

Perhaps for the same reason you might think that a dad should be the last person to be awarded custody of a child: inaccurate beliefs about gender. If I have read correctly, at least one of our brilliant states in the USA thinks that children with an unfit mom will need another female to take care of them since dads are *not okay* until children are at least seven years of age.

Can I please use more profanity to call those amazingly ignorant morons what they really are? I'll be willing to take bets that a state like that has some of the highest statistical rates of gender and race discrimination. That also means a state like that probably falls well behind its peers in competitive measurements. Ironically, such states are run by those who are probably the first to argue against proactive ideas like affirmative action too.

Forces that want women held back in their kitchens and thus, at the mercy of their potentially cheating husbands, god forbid, are also keeping women dependant on child support when a divorce occurs. Why allow women to have the real power and autonomy when they are obviously still fine with suckling the teats of men?

The point I am making here is that not only are kids getting psychologically slaughtered by every-other-weekend custody arrangements, and not only are women being treated unfairly by being encouraged to stay on the teats of their ex-husbands, but men are actually being positioned to stay miserably disconnected from their kids *and* their spousal partners. Why? So that they can conquer the world of sports, business, and mistresses or whatever else they are conditioned to seek.

Women conquer the kitchen and the childrearing; men conquer the rest of the world. How nice and convenient for all involved, right?

Well, of course while your husband's are out conquering the world, I suppose some of you MILFs (or desperate housewives) may as well enjoy *being the conquest* of the man next door, or perhaps the boss, or even a customer at the job where you probably aren't paid enough.

In a divorce situation, what is it that makes us do what we do with ourselves, and our kids and our exes? Surely it is our beliefs that compel our decisions. And the courts will often keep the peace of our beautiful system, where females depend on men for almost everything monetary. That's the way it's supposed to be, after all.

ENTER MR. MOM

The greatest thing that ever happened to me as a dad occurred when I was still married to Shauna. Circumstances forced me into taking care of my kids while Mom was working her lousy job at the gas station up the street. I want to be clear that I think couples that never see each other due to the desire to save the cash of paying for childcare, are begging for trouble. Alternating schedules to tag team with kids is neglectful of our human need for routine intimacy. It can be a HUGE mistake. Take my word on that one.

Nevertheless, I didn't really understand the implications of taking care of my kids until I actually was forced into it.

Why is that?

Nobody really expected me to take care of the kids until I had to, or at least that's what I *had thought* all along and wasn't saying.

IN NO WAY READY, AT FIRST

Now I need to be honest here. At first, I failed miserably at taking care of the kids. I had no clue what I was doing, not to mention I was dead tired. Meanwhile, Mommy worked difficult hours at the convenience store. She was doing something almost equally difficult. Her challenge was to begin acclimating to adult peer interaction instead of the demanding little kids in that depressing house. I am not saying that Shauna was happy at work either; in fact, she was often miserable, but at least she was out of the house and away from the kids for short periods of time. Even though she was frequently exhausted, she quickly learned that *there is* a life outside of the kitchen. Shhhh! If you didn't know that then just ignore what you just read.

Meanwhile, Daddy was learning what the sink and stove looked like. Even the highchair looked different when Mom was nowhere around to handle things. I was a mess at the time, but I began to do something that I hadn't ever known was possible. Instead of talking about my bond with my kids, I actually began to experience something that went beyond the superficial. I found myself headlong in the nearly impossible task of parenting small children. My time to rest and do what I wanted or needed to do…was seemingly *gone*.

A "BLACKS" AND "WHITES" ANGLE

I think that current events make great connecting analogies when trying to establish a general observatory point about why things are the way they are. Take Barack Obama for example.

I had no idea of the true honest-to-god logical thinking challenges that some of my friends and family suffer with, until I told them that I escaped my conservative voting pattern and voted for Obama. They went nuts. Now I don't allow people I love to attack me, without explaining the beliefs behind the attack. In a nutshell, I learned that many of them were nervous about a nonwhite president, though they hid behind policy issues. Personally, I find many of Obama's positions to be irreconcilable with my own beliefs, but that's pretty normal for me. I almost always struggle to get everything I want in a party-fed candidate.

To those who were critical of my voting choice and who demonstrated racial issues with trusting someone of nonwhite skin color, I had my own question.

I would ask, "So you think that the way to solve the statistical criminal disproportion in some minority communities is to toss another *old white man* in office for all of America's nonwhite children to see? That has already been tried." Not to mention the international community's awareness of our national hypocrisy. They see how our government reflects a culture of minority oppression, and it matters.

Do you see how my point relates to this chapter? We illogically think that somehow a more balanced generation of dads and moms will be produced by throwing more moms into single motherhood.

Really?

One way to squarely undo inaccurate social beliefs is to take progressive and aggressive steps that would fairly enable those in doubt to prove something. **It can be done**, even by a *negro* in the White House, even by a dad at home with the kids, even by a mom in charge of a corporation. Shall I go on?

Mindsets shift and things begin to fix *themselves* at a rapid pace when American society is confronted with successful minorities. You might be asking, "Well, why haven't more people with black skin color run for president in the past?" Not enough people believed black citizens could make it to the Oval Office or do the job effectively.

Belief.

Things begin to fix themselves when people allow challenges to their belief system. Interestingly enough, sometimes an oppressed human must also overcome confidence issues before realizing success. Some of you know about the concept of *self-fulfilling prophecy*. It's real and it doesn't help our nation be more competitive in business or foreign diplomacy. Some of our nation's social traditions are so outdated that they could soon destroy our ability to protect even the most basic resources. We _must_ compete in business. We _must_ be ethically **united** on basic common sense issues and we must _work_ **as a team**. I am not in favor of losing our national values of competitiveness and pride for work done right. Socialistic ideals are pleasant to consider, but they can also remove basic human drive to be *more efficient* with resources and *increasingly effective* at achieving necessary goals. Having said that, as a nation, we also can't afford to maintain a culture of minority oppression. Our strength is now depending on our ability to work as a diverse group of talented individuals.

In terms of effectiveness, we unleash unfathomable capacities when we start seeing the truth. Women have been left to childrearing alone because it's difficult work. So long as men can pawn off such difficult tasks on women, why wouldn't we? It's far easier to work with adults than it is infants, toddlers and developing children.

Don't you see it?

Some of the most brilliant minds have been hidden in our homes raising children while less qualified husbands have been "taking charge" outside of the home. This is not to say that raising children is less important than any other type of social contribution. Although, I am not sure how a mind poised for physics or chemistry will be fully challenged with making infant formula. Is it possible that medical breakthroughs have been missed in such arbitrary female career assignments?

Yes. It is a certainty.

Just because you might have been thinking that there was something broken in Black females, Hispanic men, or moms in general, doesn't make it true at all. In fact, we have been betraying our national interests by constricting talent all around us.

Ask yourself a more narrowing question: How many individuals have been hurt when decisions are not being founded on accurate beliefs?

Socially, we have been reinforcing the oppression of females by cultivating inaccurate beliefs about dads and moms. In fact, we have been convincing women that a female's identity depends on childrearing success while men are somehow looked at as *deficient* in parenting. With such a divisive social pattern, why should women want to realize the startling truth? Men have been capable of nurturing kids the whole time. Somehow however, *the whole* of female identity has been designed to require that men "can't perform" what women *can* with regard to baby making, and household duties like childrearing.

Never mind that women are actually just as capable as men are at running companies, *starting* companies, or making great money at satisfying jobs. Well perhaps women won't make as much as their male peers, not according to statistics; BUT if they want to, they can join the rest of us liberal nutjobs in fighting the battle of equal-compensation rights for women. God I am such an activist aren't I? My question is, why in the hell aren't you? You have to live in this mess. Why not clean it up?

The point is that so long as women don't understand that they are perhaps *more* capable of career and educational success, then wouldn't it just ruin their sense of worth to admit that men can actually share the traditionally female role responsibilities? Now I know men can't produce babies from beer bellies, but they are actually extremely emotionally capable. In fact, according to leading anthropologist Helen Fisher's 2004 book, *Why We Love,* studies have proven that a man's testosterone level drops just by picking up a baby. So you do the math.

Historically, what motive would men as a social-group have to convince women that females are only valuable in the kitchen, with the kids, or in lower-paying jobs? Did God tell men to teach women this?

People, this is scary stuff. It reminds me of something right out of the History Channel's "Jonestown Massacre" coverage.

CHALLENGING CONSIDERATIONS

Personally, I would start by considering if any of these observations I am making actually add up to an honest summary of why you think the way you do. I would go back and start challenging what you have been taught about your value as a man or woman and quickly redo the math. The truth is though, no matter how much you tell someone afraid of spiders that a few particular household spiders are harmless, they will still run the other way when they see _any_ spider won't they?

I have a few more questions.

If dads were afforded the same physical visitation benefits as moms, would the dads actually be able to cook, clean, and nurture the kids (after the normal learning curve of course)?

_____

_____

_____

_____

If dads were treated with the exact same respect that moms are in court, how would moms feel?

_____

_____

_____

_____

What if it was a lot more difficult to convince a judge that a dad is "unfit?"

_____

_____

_____

_____

If you are a man reading this, are you too much of a "man" to not do some laundry, dishes and other childcare responsibilities? What if it meant getting to see your kids off in the morning for school half of the time? Are you so materialistic that you wouldn't give up your ladder climbing career, if need be, so that you can actually accommodate the kids' schedules? Are you worried about "wasting time" by showing up for parent-teacher conferences? Dr. Appointments? Are you *so afraid* of giving your ex-wife an opportunity to easily date someone else, that you would want her stuck with the kids more?

MALE DILEMMAS

Some dads can sometimes stare at the last section a little too long. Again, men are often simply not used to having the same child rearing expectations tossed on their schedule, are they? I think its time to change that. In fact, that time is way overdue.

Men, you will soon be learning what it means to really take care of kids rather than playing house while Mom works her fucking ass off doing the things that you thought you needed a woman to do. That's right. I used to tell myself that I was different too. Even now, I *still* have to parent my children *on purpose* because of the constant struggle to think that I have a world to conquer.

Old habits die hard, but your kids need you to get some things more aligned with the *real world*. You are not Superman. You are a dad. Changing one dirty diaper a day is not an accomplishment. That doesn't even touch the radar of the true task at hand.

YES. You can do it.

YES. You will do it if you're smart. I have been challenging moms to listen to you. Are you sure you can listen to a mom? You have probably done a horrible job at it in the past, so it's hard to believe that you could pull it off now.

Moral Rights

Moms and Dads both have rights to certain legal opportunities. This chapter involves rhetorical questions to provoke serious thinking about **how you manage** those legal opportunities.

Many Things to Consider

Is it moral to take certain legal opportunities if it means the kids or one of the parents get emotionally screwed in the process? Is it possible to arrange divorce papers to protect both parents from unfair situations? Is it possible to sit down like adults and discuss the actual realities of what the family will look like after the divorce, including the financial situation of both Mom and Dad? Though not advisable, is it possible to perform a do-it-yourself divorce online and without an attorney? Are attorneys or divorce mediators good hourly resources to verify that a do-it-yourself agreement fairly protects <u>both</u> parents? Is it possible to use an attorney for the entire non-contested divorce without screwing up your coparenting situation? Is it possible to arrange for a vehicle payment to be paid, or some other type of financial negotiation to level out the financial playing field, rather than depending on child-support? Is child support even needed in a 50/50 custody situation?

What would it mean to be 100% responsible for your kids but actually have 50% of your time freed up? Could you then have the freedom to rest? What about time to explore new things like college, dating, or activities you had been unable to perform in the unhealthy marriage?

Please answer a few more questions.

Should a dad automatically have more legal rights than a mom? Do you need to explain your answer? Please do. I'll give you one line to do it.

_____

Should a mom automatically have more legal rights than a dad? Need to explain?

_____

Are you going to allow a court or attorney to basically make choices for you? Need to explain?

_____

WHERE DO THE KIDS FIT IN HERE?

This section is easy…and hard. The following questions are about the needs of children. In a way, these questions ask about your children's rights, or what you believe about your kids.

Do the kids still need to feel like they are part of a family, even if Mom and Dad get divorced? Please explain.

_____

_____

_____

_____

_____

Should a younger child be put in a position to decide which parent he or she wants to live with?

_____

_____

_____

_____

_____

_____

_____

Are children mature enough to judge their own developmental needs?

_____

_____

_____

_____

_____

_____

_____

Using a divorce mediator if needed, what might your divorced family look like with standard every-other-weekend visitation schedule?

_____

_____

_____

_____

_____

_____

_____

_____

_____

_____

_____

_____

_____

_____

Using a divorce mediator if needed, what might your divorced family look like with shared 50/50 visitation with both parents?

_____

_____

_____

_____

_____

_____

_____

_____

_____

_____

_____

_____

_____

_____

_____

_____

SHARED PARENTING BASICS

Here is a list of benefits to a 50/50 *physical* custody arrangement. It allows for a creative visitaion schedule, but I personally would not recommend anything other than split-week schedules or bi-weekly schedules. All of my trial and error would suggest that you stick to the schedules provided in the next chapter.

Note that both parents must remain in the same school district due to the school bus routes. In my divorce agreement, any move to another school district requires that the coparents *negotiate* moves together <u>as a family</u>. That means that relocations must be mutual and agreed upon prior to either parent moving. I have actually done it twice, and in both cases, the kids' best interests were discussed throughout the entire negotiation. This mutalally benificial custody arrangement is normally <u>so</u> solid, that negotiations in almost anything are easier.

There is something for both parents to lose if a 50/50 Physical Custody situation fails. 50/50 visiatation schedules include priceless benefits for kids and <u>both</u> parents once everyone is accustomed to the schedule.

NOTICE SOME OF THE BENEFITS BELOW

The kids win because...

- They normally have <u>both</u> Mom and Dad at some point during each week.
- They still feel the family and are still part of a team.
- Kids might complain some at first, but eventually the schedule becomes a miraculous part of their security due to the equal access to *both* parents- a priceless developmental resource.

- Kids normally get some help from both parents in homework, and often parents differ in skills.

- Both parents will almost always know about the school clothes situation (kids certainly can rapidly outgrow *and* ruin clothes)

- The kids do not have to suffer from missing another parent or feeling depressed about missing a parent that was in their life prior to the divorce.

The parents win because...

- Both parents get a scheduled breather to relax more.

- Both parents have wiggle room to get started on "starting over."

- Both parents can take scheduled adult-only vacations (even during the schoolyear!).

- Time is regularly available to deal with unrelated personal issues, without risking child neglect.

- Parents *share* denist and doctor visits so one person is not stuck calling out of work every time.

- Holidays are still alternated. While this guarentees you will have some holiday time with your kids, it also allows you to make longer, more extensive trips without trying to entertain the kids for the whole trip (or refereeing their fighting).

- There is a lot more time for either parent to try something new- college, business or new hobbies.

- For the coparents, it can feel like a very effective family team, only without the marriage drama.

- Neither parent has to keep explaining to the children about why the visiation schedule is so unfair.

- It most cases, it can force the divorced adults to regularly face the other coparent, which over months or years, can help correct the typical confused or strained feelings divorced couples face. This particular benifit is priceless to psychological development and hopefully to social development as well.

SCHEDULES EXAMPLES

Schedule examples are in the next chapter.

Schedules Examples

Simple Bi-Weekly Schedule

Let's start with the easiest schedule, the biweekly schedule. This pretty much never changes. I recommend this for kids who are accustomed to the divorce or are a little older (ages six and up). Younger children tend to do better with a split-week rather than this bi-weekly plan

The Bi-Weekly Schedule						
Month						
SUNDAY	MONDAY	TUESDAY	WEDNESDAY	THURSDAY	FRIDAY	SATURDAY
m	m	m	m	m	m	m
d	d	d	d	d	d	d
m	m	m	m	m	m	m
d	d	d	d	d	d	d

SPLIT-WEEK SCHEDULE- A

The split-week is a little trickier, but it should basically alternate between Dad covering the weekends on one month and Mom on the next month. Again, this schedule is a perfect solution for many sensitive reasons; however, it can be a little more challenging at first due to the change-ups in midweek. Does it work, though? It DOES work, and it is very useful when the bi-weekly schedule is just too long for kids to go without seeing the other parent. The much easier solution will be migrating permanently to the bi-weekly as soon as the family is ready, but do not rush into a bi-weekly schedule. I cannot stress this enough! There is a certain feeling of instability to the split-week schedule but it does something very unique. It allows for everyone to acclimate to the divorce and the joint mission of both households. It also keeps separation anxiety from interrupting child development at critical stages. You are the parents, and you must collaborate together to learn when the children are ready to make the switch.

The Split-Week Schedule-A

MONTH

SUNDAY	MONDAY	TUESDAY	WEDNESDAY	THURSDAY	FRIDAY	SATURDAY
m	m	m	m	d	d	d
m	m	m	d	d	d	d
m	m	m	m	d	d	d
m	m	m	d	d	d	d

SPLIT-WEEK SCHEDULE- B

On the previous schedule, Mom has weekends off on the "A-Month." Dad will have weekends off in the "B-Month," as illustrated below:

The Split-Week Schedule-B

MONTH						
SUNDAY	MONDAY	TUESDAY	WEDNESDAY	THURSDAY	FRIDAY	SATURDAY
d	d	d	d	m	m	m
d	d	d	m	m	m	m
d	d	d	m	m	m	m
d	d	d	d	m	m	m

JUST THE FACTS

Fiction: Moms and dads should first win a national character contest before they are a good enough example to raise the kids 50% of the time. **Fact:** Kids need Dad and Mom both equally. Requiring someone to have perfect character is an adult's immature manipulation. The kids will be fine with a parent of average character.

STRONG THOUGHTS ON ADULTRY AND "REVENGE"

Let's talk about adultery for a moment. I think "cheating" is typical, common, and basic to American marriage. It is estimated that 30 to 60% of all married adults have participated in an adulterous relationship. That's pretty common if you ask me.

Do you recommend that we remove custody rights from 50% of Americans simply because they have an affair or multiple affairs? Do you seriously believe that adultery makes someone an unfit parent? What if someone is a vegetarian? Or not a vegetarian? Isn't that a moral issue?

If you think that adultery is grounds for divorce, then *for you*, it can be an excellent reason to divorce. I personally think that infidelity can be an excellent confrontation with real-life; a signal of romantic trouble that shouldn't be ignored. So for me, it's the start of real problem solving, which *may* include a breakup. For you, it might be the *final straw*.

Many people use adultery as the only reason for leaving someone. They say, "I just can't trust you anymore." In reality, there are probably multiple reasons for the breakup. Adultery just makes it easier to skip the other facts, point a finger, and end the marriage.

If cheating *was* involved in your marriage, it has NOTHING to do with your ex's parenting ability and has EVERYTHING to do with the romantic friendship you shared (or didn't share) with your ex. You are no longer in a romantic relationship with the other parent. The issue is no longer relevant.

Humans are VERY sexually driven creatures and people who shout about their morality are the first to distrust in romantic situations. I feel that those people who are vibrant, alert, engaged, and with a typical sex drive, will be hard-pressed to avoid adultery, though it is possible. Nobody wants to hear that. Most folks want to play the "character card."

I think that people tend to behave in different ways when in different circumstances. That's why the main science to monogamy is learning the honest truth about what constitutes circumstantial vulnerability.

I am not condoning infidelity. I simply understand it. You should too.

Adults, who **consensually** have sex with other adults, whether married or not, are doing just *that:* having sex. Sex has no relation to a custody situation unless one would sacrifice the emotional and mental health of kids in order to rub an affair in an ex's face. After all, the adultery hurt your feelings, right? Just break up, be adults about the incompatibility and begin moving on.

Not all future partners will cheat. Keep in mind that the personality you are attracted to may be more open to mischief, so the intimacy in future relationships will need to be much stronger. To reduce surprises, you might have to explore ALL of someone in order to establish something you can trust, but also not get bored of. Intimacy is the answer, but it requires a realistic approach. You might not be ready for that yet.

Fiction: Dads can't learn to nurture kids.

Fact: Dads are highly capable of nurturing when they are expected to and trusted to. Sometimes, dads can be *more* nurturing than moms; and sometimes, moms can be more adventurous than dads. Many of the stereotypical gender characteristics are not accurate at all times. I have been interested when people notice how nurturing I am with my girls and my son. Dads can often be VERY soft and affectionate when the **need** and expectation is presented. As mentioned earlier, hormonal predisposition towards particular potentials are mostly noticeable <u>when</u> *circumstances permit*. There is such a thing as *Plan B*, however inconvenient.

Fiction: Your kids won't understand if you are not always with them 100% of the time.

Fact: Kids won't understand if you screw them out of equal opportunities with the other parent. Recognize that while a child may seem to get nothing "special" out of a 50/50 arrangement, they are probably getting something important on deeper levels.

Fiction: This whole thing seems confusing and strange.

Fact: Perhaps *at first* it may seem that way, but in the long run, it is a lot easier to organize your life and to begin healing from a divorce when you get some time alone to figure out your new options. Though there may be an initial gut reflex to keep your world functioning "as normal," it is far less normal to have the kids almost completely out of your coparenting partner's life. "Normal," in fact, would be acknowledging the truth of the situation and immediately beginning a respectful and *golden-rule oriented* coparenting arrangement. The benefits you can reap far outweigh the work of planting such seeds.

CONCLUSION

Something interesting to remember is that you will only get one shot at this. While you may get one or more opportunities to figure out marriages or careers, you probably will not get another opportunity to protect your children from an inhumane custody situation, at least not without a lot of expensive legal fees and unneeded confusion for your kids. There are options available to fix the problem *now*, <u>before</u> you, your children and your coparent are harmed. The snowball of one bad decision can often open up a vacuum of negative consequences that the entire family will pay dearly for. Remember to keep facts and fiction separated in this process.

In a choice of optimism, I have provided you with some blank hypothetical visitation schedule worksheets in the Appendix. You could privately fill them in with what you might do in a 50/50 child custody visitation situation. That *should be* your absolute goal. Just remember that in order to protect everyone, especially kids, neither you nor the other parent can relocate unless you move at the same time *as a family*.

Consult the other parent to find a win-win.
Since it's your life, you are allowed to consult your future coparent whenever you want. These are your kids and the other parent's kids too. It makes sense to come up with a winning plan.
See Appendix F for final thoughts.

Make better choices.

APPENDIX A: THE SURVEY

The following link is for readers to provide the author with feedback. These publications are designed to evolve in future editions through the feedback you provide.

Was the book helpful?

Was something missing?

If the author uses your feedback directly to improve a future edition, you will be provided with a fresh copy of the improved publication at no charge.

www.honestguides.com/childcustody.htm

APPENDIX B: DIVORCE AGREEMENT

A divorce agreement is the legal document containing the essential terms of a divorce. Within the agreement you will find the Child Visitation Schedule and its terms.

A court will most likely require that a divorce agreement indentify one of the parents as the primary "legal and residential custodian," thus that designated parent is "subject to" the legal and physical visitation rights of the other parent. While I don't agree with one-custodian legislation, so long as both parents are serious about making sure that the kids are healthy and safe, it probably doesn't matter which parent is identified as the custodial parent. The entire agreement must be totally understood and agreed upon or you shouldn't sign it. Did you hear me just now? Mom? Dad? If you don't agree, *never sign it*. Put your nose in the air until you both feel like it's a win-win (or a "lose-lose" in most cases). Either way, sometimes both parents end up equally screwed when a divorce occurs.

The key is a spirit of fairness, or else one of you is going to harbor bitterness. That can't be allowed to happen or you will end up with the problems that every other divorced couple have. Those couples end up blaming the other parent for almost all of their problems. Do you know divorced couples like that? It's totally ridiculous! No bitterness allowed, okay? You talk it out until something decent is coordinated. Remember, you are both adults and if the plan includes fairness, then why complain at all?

In my divorce, as a dad, I was identified as the custodial parent, and it has had ZERO impact on anything, other than my self-esteem as a dad. In our case, Shauna probably got ten times the cooperation from me just for making the gesture. It was an innocent legal "kiss on the cheek" instead of the slap on the face I could have experienced. To this day, she has me eating out of her hand. I am sure she is glad she didn't listen to the attorneys, the judge, or her family and friends (*everyone,* to be honest). Remember, those people are not coparenting with her each week- I am. And that fact makes all the difference every day of our lives in the present situation.

Back when Shauna and I were planning and discussing our entire plan (our agreement), before we ever walked into court, we found our common ground and it wasn't easy. We cried a lot. No attorneys were sitting between us to make us uncomfortable. In our coparenting choices to this day, we both still cross-reference back to those initial conversations to be sure that neither of us is trying to cheat on the decisions we negotiated. As a result, we can both look at ourselves in the mirror, and it feels good. Our kids notice too.

The real issue is whether or not the custodial parent is really a **coparent** at heart, or if they are on a power trip. Someone who might hoard the power of making medical or dental decisions alone rather than consulting the other parent would probably not be the best idea for the legal ID of "custodial parent." My kids never have decisions made about them without **full** buy-in from both Mom and Dad. We nearly **insist** on reaching mutual agreements to make sure that the best possible decisions are made. Two heads are better than one, and it feels better to know that we are not going out on limbs alone. This includes questionable movie viewing, new hairstyles, and even new piercings. (I learned that one the hard way when I got Kayla's second holes for her ears. How was I supposed to know that was a big deal? I got chewed-out for fifteen minutes, and no, I will not forget in the future.) Don't get sidetracked on the custodial designation if you can help it.

The example below includes the mother as the custodial parent but sharing a 50/50 physical visitation schedule. The wording includes the father as the petitioner but you could simply substitute the word "Petitioner" with the word "Respondent" if needed. When Shauna and I divorced, we actually went back and forth on who would be the "Respondent" and who would be the "Petitioner" and in the end, it didn't make a difference at all in terms of the execution of the fair agreement we created together.

Notice that the arrangement is a bi-weekly arrangement. As co-parents you can decide to use the split-week schedule for as long as you need to, but to protect yourselves, in the event that you have unforeseen problems with the other coparent, it is best to lock-in a final schedule that is durable (doable) on a permanent basis: the bi-weekly schedule.

Note that a divorce doesn't actually have to be rushed. If one parent needs to find another job or manage a schedule change at work, it is in your best interest to allow a reasonable amount of time (sixty days) to allow for the work schedules to align with the below visitation schedule. In the long run, a small amount of patience can go a long way for the entire agreement to remain fair and mutually satisfying.

(1)

The Petitioner-Father shall have the right to visit with the children at any time that is mutually agreeable to both parties. In the event that the parties cannot agree, the following schedule shall apply:

None of the visitation rights set out herein shall be exercised so as to place the minor children in any situation detrimental to their health, education, and welfare. The Petitioner and Respondent shall each exercise their respective rights in a wholesome atmosphere and environment, consistent with the moral and physical well being of the minor children. Neither party shall place the minor children in a position with that intent as discussed herein.

Visitation for each parent shall be every other week from 6:00 o'clock p.m. on Sunday until 6:00 o'clock p.m. on the following Sunday, commencing on Sunday after the signing of this agreement, and continuing every other week thereafter.

The parties shall alternate holidays based on agreeable terms. No party shall have the children on a particular holiday more often than once every other year. Additionally, no party shall have the children on both Thanksgiving and Christmas in the same calendar year.

Notwithstanding anything to the contrary, the Petitioner shall have the right to have the minor children visit with him on Father's Day from 6:00 o'clock p.m. on Saturday before Father's Day until 6:00 o'clock p.m. on Father's Day.

Notwithstanding anything to the contrary, the Respondent shall have the right to have the minor children visit with her on Mother's Day from 6:00 o'clock p.m. on Saturday before Mother's Day until 6:00 o'clock p.m. on Mother's Day.

Each parent shall have the right of reasonable visitation on the children's birthday. The parent not then otherwise having custody or visitation shall have the right of visitation not less than (4) hours, from 2:00 o'clock p.m. until 6:00 o'clock p.m.

The parties shall mutually agree to a schedule regarding locations to pick-up and drop-off the children for their visitations.

If the parties cannot agree to a basic understanding regarding phone calls with the children the following schedule will apply:

When the children are with one parent, the children may telephone the other parent. Either parent may speak with the children by telephone during reasonable hours, of reasonable duration, and made with reasonable frequency, no more than once per day.

Either party's visitation shall not interfere with the children's attendance during the school year. Both parties agree that they will strive to maintain residence in the same school district wherein the children attend school. In the event that either parent cannot reside in the same school district, that party agrees to provide reliable transportation to and from school with a typical travel time of no more than 15-minutes. In the event that either party desires to relocate beyond the

15-minute proximity, that party must first negotiate with the other party regarding possible relocation terms, which must include both parties relocating to a new school district. The potential relocation must be on agreed terms which must include a flexible and agreeable schedule. It is never the responsibility of either party to agree to a relocation plan, thus in the event that negotiations cannot be agreeable, relocation will fail to occur altogether and both parties will continue to maintain residence in the same school district.

Each party shall, at all times, keep the other party informed of the health and whereabouts of the children, and cooperate with each other so that the children may attend scheduled extra curricular activities.

APPENDIX C: BI-WEEKLY SCHEDULE

This alternates weekly. Dad has the kids during one week; Mom has the kids on the next week. Bi-Weekly is an advanced schedule.

The Bi-Weekly Schedule

MONTH						
SUNDAY	MONDAY	TUESDAY	WEDNESDAY	THURSDAY	FRIDAY	SATURDAY

APPENDIX D: SPLIT-WEEK "A"

This schedule is to be alternated with Split-Week Schedule "B" from the next appendix. Split-Week is a beginner's schedule.

The Split-Week Schedule-A

MONTH						
SUNDAY	MONDAY	TUESDAY	WEDNESDAY	THURSDAY	FRIDAY	SATURDAY

APPENDIX E: SPLIT-WEEK "B"

This schedule is to be alternated with Split-Week Schedule (A) from the previous appendix.

The Split-Week Schedule-B

MONTH

SUNDAY	MONDAY	TUESDAY	WEDNESDAY	THURSDAY	FRIDAY	SATURDAY

APPENDIX F: FINAL THOUGHTS

Dads and Moms...PAY ATTENTION FOR ONE LAST POINT!

I have never tried to abuse my divorce agreement or any oral agreements made with my coparent. I strongly believe that perversion or manipulation of the concepts in this book (taking the smallest shortcut) may result in a partial or total loss of coparenting stability. I would treat these concepts with more integrity and respect than you have treated anything.

You might choose to add flexibility to your plan, put it all in writing and just stick to what you both decide. If you stick to your agreements, you can't lose; however, if you can't stick to your agreements, then I wouldn't get near anything like this. This is major league ball for adults, not little league. Courts frown strongly on grownups who can't stick to their word.

So, if you are totally irresponsible, if you want to test cheating at parenting, cheating a court judgment, or cheating the need to be totally fair to the other parent, you go right ahead. You will almost certainly suffer a tremendous loss.

The good guys and good gals often *do win*.

("good" = fair)

Appendix G: Child Support Info

Shauna and I realized while reviewing our situation that we would both be lucky to even pay rent for places of our own. To keep our incomes balanced, I agreed to pay for her vehicle payment until she remarried. That balanced the money between us so that we would both be equally screwed. So I do not pay child support.

We did meet with an attorney at one point and I would have been paying over $1,000 a month had the attorney had his way and my kids would not be living with me right now 50% of the time. Once the dust settled, the family would have suffered miserably.

I enjoy paying for at least half of everything kid-related and I also pay for the kid's medical insurance. My living standards and Shauna's living standards are very similar due to the vehicle payment factor.

I have been going to college and one day I will make more money and it will not go out in child support. That would be totally unfair to me, trying to better myself, and frankly I think the idea is criminal for my situation. Shauna can go to college just as easily or with just as much difficulty as I do. After all, she has no kids for a week at a time every-other-week.

Distance Learning college degree programs are excellent if you attend a state university. There are a lot of high-priced online "colleges" that I would avoid. Stick with state programs.

I do not believe that child support is needed at all except in very rare situations where 50/50 visitation isn't possible (a dad or mom cannot stay out of jail, off of drugs, away from abusive alcohol consumption, etc.)

These difficult situations are common to lower-educated, lower-income families and since you are proactively reading a book like this, they *probably* do not fit your situation. Although, consider the occupation of typical cocaine users: attorneys, judges and politicians right?

So, I believe 50/50 is in, and child support is out. Forms of alimony are IN.

Men? Women? Attorneys? Judges? Legislators? If Mom was doing her best to support "her man" all these years and taking care of the kids while Dad went to college or climbed ANY ladder, oh he needs to pay **if** it balances the lifestyle arrangements. But not *through* child support.

It should be a fair exchange (ex.: The higher income earner pays for the other's college or other compensation arrangements can be made to temporarily accommodate a similar financial *budget*, etc) for a limited time or until the other parent remarries. Once a dad and mom have made agreements on what is fair, they should consult a legal expert on how to put it in enforceable writing.

It is unrealistic for a mom or dad to expect to maintain *the same* lifestyle since the household is now divorced and needing to split in half, and money is tighter. There should be fair financial situations to accommodate <u>each</u> parent with a *smaller* apartment or house, a *cheaper* vehicle, less frivolous spending, etc. There *was* financial strength in staying together, which is gone due to the divorce. BOTH will have to adjust to a "new and improved" reduced budget. BOTH will have opportunities to improve that budget when the dust settles and they move on. *I don't care whose fault the divorce was.* **It doesn't matter.**

APPENDIX H: ☑ CUSTODY ADVICE

Regardless of whether you are currently divorcing or wanting to challenge an unhealthy custody arrangement, this checklist is for you.

- ☐ Secure an affordable but "experienced" custody attorney.
- ☐ Immediately take residence in the same school district.
- ☐ The residence must be suitable, safe and have adequate space for you and your kids.
- ☐ Take a job that reasonably accommodates school schedules.
- ☐ If you will be off work by six p.m., secure reliable after-school care.
- ☐ Avoid all drug or violent criminal activity.
- ☐ If you have been involved in drugs, violence, or alcohol abuse you will need to seek treatment for these issue(s).
- ☐ After treatment for the issue(s), you will probably require a certified evaluation by a professional and **a solid follow-up plan**.
- ☐ Be patient and remain stable which includes not living with a new romantic partner too soon.
- ☐ Make sure you respect the custody situation of the other party, PERIOD. If you argue with the law from the beginning, you will not appear capable of working with the law later if it turns to your favor.

☐ Read about the laws in your state (see Appendix I)

☐ Read books about child custody.

☐ Be patient and be prepared to take time working through the system with your attorney. The system is sometimes slow due to many factors out of your control and the system is also cautious with changes.

☐ Stay positive.

☐ Do not go after more than 50/50 visitation. The healthy thing will often <u>not</u> be taking 100% custody. Taking more than 50/50 is unreasonable and will place a tremendous burden of proof on you and your attorney.

☐ Your task is not to make life difficult for the other parent; it is actually to simply acquire the 50% visitation that you are already morally entitled to have already.

☐ Respect the laws (has that been said?)

☐ Consult your attorney whenever you need to and do not be afraid to consult a different attorney if you have concerns about the speed of things.

☐ Use common sense and a reasonable attitude. If you are out to prove something then you are obviously not out to care for your kids. This is not a competition! Rather, this is a fair legal settlement needing to occur if you play by the rules, make the kids your number-one concern, and keep your pride in-check. Let your attorney represent "your rights," not you.

☐ Let the courts know you are interested in 50/50 physical custody ASAP. If your attorney has reservations on timing then you should probably listen. *Timing* is what your attorney could help you with the most if he or she knows something you don't know. Otherwise, **go fast** to get a legal interest loud and clear to the court.

☐ Remember that you might be fighting up against legal tradition and breaking tradition is not what legal professionals make a living doing. They support tradition and precedence. So a gracious disposition in lieu of an arrogant attitude will be your only option if you are to be seen as a reasonable "risk" worth changing something that traditionally wouldn't be changed. Make sense?

☐ Play nice with the other parent. You can be firm about your desire for 50/50 visitation without being mean, defensive or accusatory.

☐ Realize that custody laws and general procedures are supposed to protect children from angry parents and the typical emotionally disturbing fights between parents. Why? The greatest threat to shared parenting is a kid witnessing this sort of high-velocity fighting. I understand that the family courts pour rocket-fuel on the flames by manipulating our rights to parent our kids. BUT, if you don't respect this rule of *never fighting in front of the kids*, if you think your kids are old enough to handle the typical divorce conflicts, you really *don't* need to have those kids very often *until* you change your mind. Get a book on divorce research such as, *The Unexpected Legacy of Divorce* by Wallerstein. Kids need parents to be informed and sensitive to their psychological vulnerabilities. If you don't want to get into *all that,* then just do one thing and you will be fine: **never fight in front of the kids**.

APPENDIX I: THE STATE LAWS

This appendix deals with state laws. The individual summaries for each state are not comprehensive and are only included to provide you with information to discuss with your attorney. Your attorney can help you determine the law and how to best leverage it towards a 50/50 visitation schedule. In addition, laws may have changed following the publication of this book. In some state summaries, the exact text of the statute may have been simplified and/or modified to provide for easier understanding.

Notice that some states have very progressive legislation compared to the "backward" legislation of other states. This is very alarming when you consider how much control these states are using to manipulate the reinforcement of unfair and completely ignorant gender role assignments. Longitudinal research over the last twenty-five years has indicated that some of these laws might sentence children to potentially permanent *mental* and *emotional* disturbances.

Most of the information in this section was used by permission of **www.helpyourselfdivorce.com**, a very handy website loaded with information. Use the *State Custody Index List* on the next page to locate your state or review information we have located about other states. We will be revising the information regularly in future editions of this book. If you notice opportunities to make the state summaries more uniform in format, more accurate, or with improved references, please contact the author or publisher.

State Custody Law Index List

Clay H. Emerton

Alabama

Guidelines for Child Custody Under Alabama Laws.
Upon granting a divorce, the court may give the custody and education of the children of the marriage to either father or mother, as may seem right and proper, having regard to the moral character and prudence of the parents and the age and sex of the children; and pending the action, may make such orders in respect to the custody of the children as their safety and well-being may require. But in cases of abandonment of the husband by the wife, he shall have the custody of the children after they are seven years of age, if he is a suitable person to have such charge.

-From Section 30-3-1 of the Code of Alabama

Joint Custody.
It is the policy of the state of Alabama to assure that minor children have frequent and continuing contact with parents who have shown the ability to act in the best interest of their children and to encourage parents to share in the rights and responsibilities of rearing their children after the parents have separated or dissolved their marriage.

The court shall in every case consider joint custody but may award any form of custody which is determined to be in the best interest of the child. In determining whether joint custody is in the best interest of the child, the court shall consider the same factors considered in awarding sole legal and physical custody and all of the following factors:

(1) The agreement or lack of agreement of the parents on joint custody.
(2) The past and present ability of the parents to cooperate with each other and make decisions jointly.
(3) The ability of the parents to encourage the sharing of love, affection, and contact between the child and the other parent.
(4) Any history of or potential for child abuse, spouse abuse, or kidnapping.
(5) The geographic proximity of the parents to each other as this relates to the practical considerations of joint physical custody. The court may order a form of joint custody without the consent of both parents, when it is in the best interest of the child. If both parents request joint custody, the presumption is that joint custody is in the best interest of the child. Joint custody shall be granted in the final order of the court unless the court makes specific findings as to why joint custody is not granted.

-From Sections 30-3-150 and 30-3-152 of the Code of Alabama

Definitions.
The state of Alabama has defined the following terms:
(1) JOINT CUSTODY. Joint legal custody and joint physical custody.
(2) JOINT LEGAL CUSTODY. Both parents have equal rights and responsibilities for major decisions concerning the child, including, but not limited to, the education of the child, health care, and religious training. The court may designate one parent to have sole power to make certain decisions while both parents retain equal rights and responsibilities for other decisions.

(3) JOINT PHYSICAL CUSTODY. Physical custody is shared by the parents in a way that assures the child frequent and substantial contact with each parent. Joint physical custody does not necessarily mean physical custody of equal durations of time.

(4) SOLE LEGAL CUSTODY. One parent has sole rights and responsibilities to make major decisions concerning the child, including, but not limited to, the education of the child, health care, and religious training.

(5) SOLE PHYSICAL CUSTODY. One parent has sole physical custody and the other parent has rights of visitation except as otherwise provided by the court.

-From the Section 30-3-151 of the Code of Alabama

Availability of Records.
Unless otherwise prohibited by court order or statute, all records and information pertaining to the child, including, but not limited to, medical, physiological, dental, scholastic, athletic, extracurricular, and law enforcement, shall be equally available to both parents, in all types of custody arrangements.

-From Section 30-3-154 of the Code of Alabama

Alaska
Alaska's child custody laws specify a number of factors in determining custody, including the following guidelines:
(1) the physical, emotional, mental, religious, and social needs of the child;
(2) the capability and desire of each parent to meet those needs;
(3) the child's preference as to custody if the child is of sufficient age and capacity to form a preference;
(4) the love and affection existing between the child and each parent;
(5) the length of time the child has lived in a stable, satisfactory environment and the desirability of maintaining continuity;
(6) the desire and ability of each parent to allow an open and loving frequent relationship between the child and the other parent;
(7) any evidence of domestic violence, child abuse, or child neglect in the household where child custody has been proposed, or a history of violence between the parents;
(8) evidence that substance abuse by either parent or other members of the household directly affects the emotional or physical well-being of the child;
(9) other factors that the court considers pertinent in determining custody of the child.

In awarding child custody, the court may consider only those facts that directly affect the well-being of the child.

In Alaska, joint child custody is known as "shared custody". The petition for dissolution of marriage in Alaska distinguishes between legal custody and physical custody. Legal custody is who makes the decisions regarding the children, and physical custody is who the children physically reside with for the majority of the year.

Alaska statutes specifically prohibit the preference of one parent over the other in child custody proceedings. A custody determination is considered based on the "best interests of the child". If the court believes that shared custody of the child would promote frequent and continuing contact with each parent, and would be in the child's best interest, the court may award shared custody of the child - either legal, physical, or both.

In determining whether to award shared custody of a child, the court shall consider the following, in addition to the above factors:
(1) The child's preference as to custody if the child is of sufficient age and capacity to form a preference;
(2) The needs of the child;
(3) The stability of the home environment likely to be offered by each parent;
(4) The education of the child;
(5) The advantages of keeping the child in the community where the child presently resides;
(6) The optimal time for the child to spend with each parent, considering:
  (A) The actual time spent with each parent;
  (B) The proximity of each parent to the other and to the school in which the child is enrolled;
  (C) The feasibility of travel between the parents;
  (D) Special needs unique to the child that may be better met by one parent than the other;
  (E) Which parent is more likely to encourage frequent and continuing contact with the other parent;
(7) Any findings and recommendations of a neutral mediator;
(8) Any evidence of domestic violence, child abuse, or child neglect in the household where custody has been proposed, or a history of violence between the parties;
(9) Evidence that substance abuse by either parent or other members of the household directly affects the emotional or physical well-being of the child;
(10) Other factors not specifically expressed by Alaska laws that are   considered pertinent by the court.

In awarding child custody in Alaska, the court shall comply with the provisions of 25 U.S.C. 1901 - 1963 (P.L. 95-608, the Indian Child Welfare Act of 1978).

Arizona
Guidelines for Child Custody Under Arizona Laws.
(25-403)
Arizona laws require the court to determine child custody in accordance with the best interests of the child. The court shall consider all relevant factors, including the following guidelines:
1. The wishes of the child's parent or parents as to custody.
2. The wishes of the child as to custody.
3. The interaction and interrelationship of the child with the child's parent or parents, the child's siblings and any other person who may significantly affect the child's best interest.

4. The child's adjustment to home, school and community.
5. The mental and physical health of all individuals involved.
6. Which parent is more likely to allow the child frequent and meaningful continuing contact with the other parent.
7. If one parent, both parents or neither parent has provided primary care of the child.
8. The nature and extent of coercion or duress used by a parent in obtaining a child custody agreement.
9. Whether a parent has complied with the educational program regarding children and divorce that is required by Arizona laws.

Preferences of the Court.
In awarding child custody, the court may order sole custody or joint custody. The child custody laws in Arizona do not create a presumption in favor of sole custody over joint custody, or vice versa. The court, in determining custody of a child, shall not prefer one parent as custodian because of that parent's sex.

Joint Custody.
The court may award joint custody of a child if both parents agree and submit a written parenting plan and the court finds that joint custody is in the best interests of the child. The court may order joint legal custody without ordering joint physical custody.

The court may issue an order for joint custody over the objection of one of the parents if the court makes specific written findings of why joint custody is in the best interest of the child. In addition to the factors listed above in determining custody, the court will consider the following factors in determining whether joint custody is in the child's best interests:

1. The custody agreement or lack of a custody agreement by the parents regarding joint custody.
2. A parent's lack of agreement is unreasonable or is influenced by an issue not related to the best interests of the child.
3. The past, present and future abilities of the parents to cooperate in decision-making about the child to the extent required by the order of joint custody.
4. Whether the joint custody agreement is logistically possible.

Joint custody shall not be awarded if the court makes a finding of the existence of significant domestic violence or if the court finds by a preponderance of the evidence that there has been a significant history of domestic violence.

Parenting Plan.
The parents must submit a parenting plan setting out each parent's rights and responsibilities for the following:
1. The personal care of the child and for decisions in areas such as education, health care and religious training;
2. A physical custody schedule for the child, including holidays and school vacations;

3. A procedure by which proposed changes, disputes and alleged breaches may be mediated or resolved, which may include the use of conciliation services or private counseling;
4. A procedure for periodic review of the terms of the parenting plan by the parents; and
5. A statement that the parties understand that joint custody does not necessarily mean equal parenting time.

Access to Records.
Unless otherwise provided by court order or law, on reasonable request both parents are entitled to have equal access to documents and other information concerning the child's education and physical, mental, moral and emotional health including medical, school, police, court and other records. A parent who attempts to restrict the release of documents or information by the custodian without a prior court order is subject to appropriate legal sanctions.

Domestic Violence.
The court shall consider evidence of domestic violence as being contrary to the best interests of the child. If the court determines that a parent who is seeking custody of the child has committed an act of domestic violence against the other parent, there is a refutable presumption that a child custody award to the parent who committed the act of domestic violence is contrary to the best interests of the child. This presumption does not apply if both parents have committed an act of domestic violence. The court may place restrictions upon a parent who it finds has engaged in acts of domestic violence, if it finds that doing so is in the best interest of the child.

Arkansas
Jurisdiction of the Arkansas Court.
Unless grounds exist for temporary emergency jurisdiction, Arkansas Courts have jurisdiction to make an initial child-custody determination only if:
(1) this state is the home state of the child on the date of the commencement of the proceeding, or was the home state of the child within six months before the commencement of the proceeding and the child is absent from this state but a parent or person acting as a parent continues to live in this state;
(2) no other state is the home state of the child, or a court of the home state of the child has declined to exercise jurisdiction on the ground that this state is the more appropriate forum under § 9-19-207 or § 9-19-208, and:
  (A) the child and the child's parents, or the child and at least one parent or a person acting as a parent, have a significant connection with this state other than mere physical presence; and
  (B) substantial evidence is available in this state concerning the child's care, protection, training, and personal relationships;
(3) all courts having jurisdiction have declined to exercise jurisdiction on the ground that a court of this state is the more appropriate forum to determine the custody of the child; or
(4) no court of any other state would have jurisdiction.

Physical presence of, or personal jurisdiction over, a party or a child is not necessary or sufficient to make a child-custody determination.

A court of this state which has made a child-custody determination consistent with § 9-19-201 or § 9-19-203 has exclusive, continuing jurisdiction over the determination until:
(1) a court of this state determines that neither the child, nor the child and one parent, nor the child and a person acting as a parent have a significant connection with this state and that substantial evidence is no longer available in this state concerning the child's care, protection, training, and personal relationships; or
(2) a court of this state or a court of another state determines that the child, the child's parents, and any person acting as a parent do not presently reside in this state.
-From 9-19-201 and 9-19-202 of the Arkansas Code

Factors Determining Child Custody in Arkansas.
In an action for divorce, the award of custody of a child of the marriage shall be made without regard to the sex of a parent but solely in accordance with the welfare and best interest of the child. In determining the best interest of the child, the court may consider the preferences of the child if the child is of a sufficient age and capacity to reason, regardless of chronological age.

When in the best interests of a child, custody shall be awarded in such a way so as to assure the frequent and continuing contact of the child with both parents. To this effect, the circuit court may consider awarding joint custody of a child to the parents in making an order for custody. To this effect, in making an order for custody, the court may consider, among other facts, which party is more likely to allow the child or children frequent and continuing contact with the noncustodial parent and the noncustodial grandparent.

There shall be a rebuttable presumption that it is not in the best interest of the child to be placed in the custody of an abusive parent in cases where there is a finding by a preponderance of the evidence that the parent has engaged in a pattern of domestic abuse.
-From 9-13-101 of the Arkansas Code

Transfer of Custody on School Property.
In order to avoid continuing child custody controversies from involving public school personnel and to avoid disruptions to the educational atmosphere in our public schools, the transfer of a child between the child's custodial parent and noncustodial parent, when both parents are present, is prohibited from taking place on the real property of a public elementary or secondary school on normal school days during normal hours of school operations. The provisions of this section shall not prohibit one parent, custodial or noncustodial, from transporting the child to school and the other parent, custodial or noncustodial, from picking up the child from school at prearranged times on prearranged days if prior approval has been made with the school's principal.
-From 9-13-104 of the Arkansas Code

Right of Parents to School Records.

Any noncustodial parent who has been awarded visitation rights by the court with respect to a child shall, upon request, be provided a copy of the current scholastic records of such child by the school district or college attended by the child.

-From 9-13-301 of the Arkansas Code

Parenting Course.

When the parties to a divorce action have minor children residing with one or both parents, the court, prior to or after entering a decree of divorce, may require the parties to complete at least two hours of classes concerning parenting issues faced by divorced parents, or submit to mediation in regard to addressing parenting, custody, and visitation issues.

-From 9-12-322 of the Arkansas Code

California
3020.

The Legislature finds and declares that it is the public policy of this state to assure that the health, safety, and welfare of children shall be the court's primary concern in determining the best interest of children when making any orders regarding the physical or legal custody or visitation of children. The Legislature further finds and declares that the perpetration of child abuse or domestic violence in a household where a child resides is detrimental to the child.

The Legislature finds and declares that it is the public policy of this state to assure that children have frequent and continuing contact with both parents after the parents have separated or dissolved their marriage, or ended their relationship, and to encourage parents to share the rights and responsibilities of child rearing in order to effect this policy, except where the contact would not be in the best interest of the child, as provided in Section 3011.

3040.

Custody should be granted in the following order of preference according to the best interest of the child as provided in
Sections 3011 and 3020:

(1) To both parents jointly pursuant to Chapter 4 (commencing with Section 3080) or to either parent. In making an order granting custody to either parent, the court shall consider, among other factors, which parent is more likely to allow the child frequent and continuing contact with the noncustodial parent, consistent with Section 3011 and 3020, and shall not prefer a parent as custodian because of that parent's sex. The court, in its discretion, may require the parents to submit to the court a plan for the implementation of the custody order.

(2) If to neither parent, to the person or persons in whose home the child has been living in a wholesome and stable environment.

(3) To any other person or persons deemed by the court to be suitable and able to provide adequate and proper care and guidance for the child.

(b) This section establishes neither a preference nor a presumption for or against joint legal custody, joint physical custody, or sole custody, but allows the court and the family the widest discretion to choose a parenting plan that is in the best interest of the child.

3041.

(a) Before making an order granting custody to a person or persons other than a parent, over the objection of a parent, the court shall make a finding that granting custody to a parent would be detrimental to the child and that granting custody to the nonparent is required to serve the best interest of the child. Allegations that parental custody would be detrimental to the child, other than a statement of that ultimate fact, shall not appear in the pleadings. The court may, in its discretion, exclude the public from the hearing on this issue.

(b) Subject to subdivision (d), a finding that parental custody would be detrimental to the child shall be supported by clear and convincing evidence.

(c) As used in this section, "detriment to the child" includes the harm of removal from a stable placement of a child with a person who has assumed, on a day-to-day basis, the role of his or her parent, fulfilling both the child's physical needs and the child's psychological needs for care and affection, and who has assumed that role for a substantial period of time. A finding of detriment does not require any finding of unfitness of the parents.

(d) Notwithstanding subdivision (b), if the court finds by a preponderance of the evidence that the person to whom custody may be given is a person described in subdivision (c), this finding shall constitute a finding that the custody is in the best interest of the child and that parental custody would be detrimental to the child absent a showing by a preponderance of the evidence to the contrary.

3041.5.

(a) In any custody or visitation proceeding brought under this part, as described in Section 3021, or any guardianship proceeding brought under the Probate Code, the court may order any person who is seeking custody of, or visitation with, a child who is the subject of the proceeding to undergo testing for the illegal use of controlled substances and the use of alcohol if there is a judicial determination based upon a preponderance of evidence that there is the habitual, frequent, or continual illegal use of controlled substances or the habitual or continual abuse of alcohol by the parent, legal custodian, person seeking guardianship, or person seeking visitation in a guardianship. This evidence may include, but may not be limited to, a conviction within the last five years for the illegal use or possession of a controlled substance.

The court shall order the least intrusive method of testing for the illegal use of controlled substances or the habitual or continual abuse of alcohol by either or both parents, the legal custodian, person seeking guardianship, or person seeking visitation in a guardianship. If substance abuse testing is ordered by the court, the testing shall be performed in conformance with procedures and standards established by the United States Department of Health and Human Services for drug testing of federal employees. The parent, legal custodian, person seeking guardianship, or person seeking visitation in a guardianship who has undergone drug testing shall have the right to a hearing, if requested, to challenge a positive test result. A positive test result, even if challenged and upheld, shall not, by itself, constitute grounds for an adverse custody or guardianship decision. Determining the best interests of the child requires weighing all relevant factors. The court shall also consider any reports provided to the court pursuant to the Probate Code. The results of this testing shall be confidential, shall be maintained as a sealed record in the court file, and may not be released to any person except the court, the parties, their attorneys, the Judicial council (until completion of its authorized study of the testing process) and any person to whom the court expressly grants access by written order made with prior notice to all parties. Any person who has access to the test results may not disseminate copies or disclose information about the test results to any person other than a person who is authorized to receive the test results pursuant to this section. Any breach of the confidentiality of the test results shall be punishable by civil sanctions not to exceed two thousand five hundred dollars ($2,500). The results of the testing may not be used for any purpose, including any criminal, civil, or administrative proceeding, except to assist the court in determining, for purposes of the proceeding, the best interest of the child pursuant to Section 3011, and the content of the order or judgment determining custody or visitation. The court may order either party, or both parties, to pay the costs of the drug or alcohol testing ordered pursuant to this section. As used in this section, "controlled substances" has the same meaning as defined in the California Uniform Controlled Substances Act, Division 10 (commencing with Section 11000) of the Health and Safety Code.

(b) This section shall remain in effect only until January 1, 2013, and as of that date is repealed, unless a later enacted statute, that is enacted before January 1, 2013, deletes or extends that date.

3042.

(a) If a child is of sufficient age and capacity to reason so as to form an intelligent preference as to custody, the court shall consider and give due weight to the wishes of the child in making an order granting or modifying custody.

(b) In addition to the requirements of subdivision (b) of Section 765 of the Evidence Code, the court shall control the examination of the child witness so as to protect the best interests of the child.

The court may preclude the calling of the child as a witness where the best interests of the child so dictate and may provide alternative means of obtaining information regarding the child's preferences.

Colorado
Intent of Colorado Legislatures.

(14-10-124)

Colorado laws state that it is in the best interest of all parties to encourage frequent and continuing contact between each parent and the minor children of the marriage after the parents have separated or dissolved their marriage. In order to effectuate this goal, Colorado laws and lawmakers urge parents to share the rights and responsibilities of child rearing and to encourage the love, affection, and contact between the children and the parents.

Parenting Plan.
In cases involving child custody (whether contested or uncontested), both parties must submit a parenting plan or plans for the court's approval that shall address both physical custody and visitation, and the allocation of decision-making responsibilities. If no parenting plan is submitted or if the court does not approve a submitted parenting plan, the court, on its own motion, shall formulate a parenting plan that shall address physical custody and visitation and the allocation of decision-making responsibilities.

Colorado Laws on Best Interest of the Child.
The court shall determine the allocation of parental responsibilities, including physical custody and visitation, and decision-making responsibilities, in accordance with the best interests of the child giving paramount consideration to the physical, mental, and emotional conditions and needs of the child. In determining the best interests of the child for purposes of custody, the court shall consider all relevant factors, including the following guidelines under Colorado laws:
1. The wishes of the child's parents as to custody;
2. The wishes of the child if he or she is sufficiently mature to express reasoned and independent preferences as to the custody and visitation schedule;
3. The interaction and interrelationship of the child with his or her parents, his or her siblings, and any other person who may significantly affect the child's best interests;
4. The child's adjustment to his or her home, school, and community;
5. The mental and physical health of all individuals involved, except that a disability alone shall not be a basis to deny or restrict parenting time;
6. The ability of the parties to encourage the sharing of love, affection, and contact between the child and the other party;
7. Whether the past pattern of involvement of the parties with the child reflects a system of values, time commitment, and mutual support;
8. The physical proximity of the parties to each other as this relates to the practical considerations of parenting time;
9. Whether one of the parties has been a perpetrator of child abuse or neglect, which shall be supported by credible evidence;
10. Whether one of the parties has been a perpetrator of spouse abuse, which factor shall be supported by credible evidence; and
11. The ability of each party to place the needs of the child ahead of his or her own needs.

Legal Custody Laws.
The court, upon the motion of either party or its own motion, shall allocate the decision-making responsibilities between the parties based upon the best interests of the child. The court may award decision-making responsibilities (legal custody) solely to one parent or jointly between the two parents. In determining the best

interests of the child for purposes of allocating decision-making responsibilities, the court shall consider, in addition to the factors listed above, the following:

1. Credible evidence of the ability of the parties to cooperate and to make decisions jointly;
2. Whether the past pattern of involvement of the parties with the child reflects a system of values, time commitment, and mutual support that would indicate an ability as mutual decision makers to provide a positive and nourishing relationship with the child;
3. Whether an allocation of mutual decision-making responsibility on any one or a number of issues will promote more frequent or continuing contact between the child and each of the parties;
4. Whether one of the parties has been a perpetrator of child abuse or neglect that is supported by credible evidence. If the court makes a finding of fact that one of the parties has been a perpetrator of child abuse or neglect, then it shall not be in the best interests of the child to allocate mutual decision-making with respect to any issue over the objection of the other party or the representative of the child;
5. Whether one of the parties has been a perpetrator of spouse abuse that is supported by credible evidence. If the court makes a finding of fact that one of the parties has been a perpetrator of spouse abuse, then joint custody over the objection of the other party shall not be in the best interests of the child, unless the court finds that the parties are able to make shared decisions about their children without physical confrontation and in a place and manner that is not a danger to the abused party or the child.

The court shall not consider conduct of a party that does not affect that party's relationship to the child, and shall not presume that any person is better able to serve the best interests of the child because of that person's sex. If a party is absent or leaves home because of spouse abuse by the other party, such absence or leaving shall not be a factor in determining the best interests of the child.

Medical Emergencies.
In the event of a medical emergency, either party shall be allowed to obtain necessary medical treatment for the minor child or children without being in violation of the order allocating decision-making responsibility or in contempt of court.

Connecticut
Child Custody Guidelines.
In making or modifying any order with respect to custody or visitation, the court shall be guided by the best interests of the child, giving consideration to the wishes of the child if the child is of sufficient age and capable of forming an intelligent preference, provided in making the initial order the court may take into consideration the causes for dissolution of the marriage if such causes are relevant in a determination of the best interests of the child.

-From Section 46b-56 of the Connecticut Statutes.

Rights to Records.
A parent not granted custody of a minor child shall not be denied the right of access

to the academic, medical, hospital or other health records of such minor child unless otherwise ordered by the court for good cause shown.

-From Section 46b-56 of the Connecticut Statutes.

Court's Jurisdiction.
To enter a custody order for a child, the court must have jurisdiction over the child. The court has jurisdiction if one of the following applies:
(1) This state is the home state of the child on the date of the commencement of the child custody proceeding. "Home state" means the state in which a child lived with a parent or person acting as a parent for at least six consecutive months immediately before the commencement of a child custody proceeding. In the case of a child less than six months old, the term means the state in which the child lived from birth with any such parent or person acting as a parent. A period of temporary absence of any such person is counted as part of the period;
(2) This state was the home state of the child within six months of the commencement of the child custody proceeding, the child is absent from the state, and a parent or a person acting as a parent continues to reside in this state;
(3) A court of another state does not have jurisdiction under subdivisions (1) or (2) above, the child and at least one parent or person acting as a parent have a significant connection with this state other than mere physical presence, and there is substantial evidence available in this state concerning the child's care, protection, training and personal relationships;
(4) A court of another state which is the home state of the child has declined to exercise jurisdiction on the ground that this state is the more appropriate forum, the child and at least one parent or person acting as a parent have a significant connection with this state other than mere physical presence, and there is substantial evidence available in this state concerning the child's care, protection, training and personal relationships;
(5) All courts having jurisdiction under subdivisions (1) to (4), inclusive, have declined jurisdiction on the ground that a court of this state is the more appropriate forum to determine custody; or
(6) No court of any other state would have jurisdiction under subdivisions (1) to (5), inclusive.

-From Sec. 46b-115a of the Connecticut Statutes.

Delaware
Child Custody Guidelines.
The Court will determine legal and physical custody for a child in accordance with the best interests of the child. In determining the best interests of the child, the Court shall consider all relevant factors including:
(1) The wishes of the child's parent or parents as to his or her custody and residential arrangements;
(2) The wishes of the child as to his or her custodian(s) and residential arrangements;
(3) The interaction and interrelationship of the child with his or her parents, grandparents, siblings, persons cohabiting in the relationship of husband and wife with a parent of the child, any other residents of the household or persons who may significantly affect the child's best interests;

(4) The child's adjustment to his or her home, school and community;

(5) The mental and physical health of all individuals involved;

(6) Past and present compliance by both parents with their rights and responsibilities to their child; and

(7) Evidence of domestic violence.

Access to Records.

Each parent has the right to receive, on request, from the other parent, all material information concerning the child's progress in school, medical treatment, significant developments in the child's life, school activities and conferences, special religious events, and other activities in which parents may wish to participate. Each parent and child also has a right to reasonable access to the other by telephone or mail.

However, the Court can restrict the rights of a child or a parent if it finds, after a hearing, that the exercise of such rights would endanger a child's physical health or significantly impair his or her emotional development.

-From § 727 of the Delaware Code.

Additional Information.

The Court won't presume that a parent, because of his or her sex, is better qualified than the other parent to have legal or physical custody of the child. It also won't consider conduct of a proposed custodian that doesn't affect his or her relationship with the child.

-From § 722 of the Delaware Code.

Florida
Joint Legal Custody and Florida Laws.

The courts show preference for shared parental responsibility (joint legal custody) in Florida Statute 1.13(2)(b)1: "It is the public policy of this state to assure that each minor child has frequent and continuing contact with both parents after the parents separate or divorce, and to encourage parents to share the rights and responsibilities and joys of childrearing. After considering all relevant facts, the father of the child shall be given the same consideration as the mother in determining the primary residence of a child, irrespective of the age or sex of the child."

...and in Florida Statute 61.13(2)(b): "The court shall order that the parental responsibility for a minor child be shared by both parents unless the court finds that shared parental responsibility (joint legal custody) would be detrimental to the child..."

Florida Laws on Best Interest of the Child.

61.13(3)

When awarding child custody in Florida, the court will consider all factors affecting the welfare and interests of the child, including but not limited to:

a. The parent who is more likely to allow the child frequent and continuing contact with the non-custodial parent.

b. The love, affection, and other emotional ties existing between the parents and the child.

c. The capacity and disposition of the parents to provide the child with food, clothing, medical care, and other material needs.

d. The length of time the child has lived in a stable, satisfactory environment and the desirability of maintaining continuity.

e. The permanence, as a family unit, of the existing or proposed custodial home.

f. The moral fitness of the parents.

g. The mental and physical health of the parents.

h. The home, school, and community record of the child.

i. The reasonable preference of the child as to custody, if the court deems the child to be of sufficient intelligence, understanding, and experience to express a preference.

j. The willingness and ability of each parent to facilitate and encourage a close and continuous parent-child relationship between the child and the other parent.

k. Evidence that any party has knowingly provided false information to the court regarding a domestic violence proceeding.

l. Evidence of domestic violence or child abuse.

m. Any other fact not specifically expressed in these laws that the court considers to be relevant.

Parenting Course in Divorce.
A parenting course is required by Florida laws for all couples with children who obtain a divorce in Florida.

Georgia
Jurisdiction.
In order for a court to decide custody of your children, whether by agreement of the spouses or by decision of the court, that court must have jurisdiction. Except as otherwise provided in Code Section 19-9-64, a court of the state of Georgia has jurisdiction to make an initial child custody determination only if:

(1) Georgia is the home state of the child on the date of the commencement of the proceeding, or was the home state of the child within six months before the commencement of the proceeding and the child is absent from the state of Georgia but a parent or person acting as a parent continues to live in the state of Georgia; ['Home state' means the state in which a child lived with a parent or a person acting as a parent for at least six consecutive months immediately before the commencement of a child custody proceeding. In the case of a child less than six months of age, the term means the state in which the child lived from birth with any of the persons mentioned. A period of temporary absence of any of the mentioned persons is part of the period.]

(2) A court of another state does not have jurisdiction under paragraph (1) of this subsection, or a court of the home state of the child has declined to exercise jurisdiction on the ground that Georgia is the more appropriate forum under Code Section 19-9-67 or 19-9-68 and:

(A) The child and the child's parents, or the child and at least one parent or a person acting as a parent, have a significant connection with Georgia other than mere physical presence; and

(B) Substantial evidence is available in Georgia concerning the child's care, protection, training, and personal relationships;

(3) All courts having jurisdiction under paragraph (1) or (2) of this subsection have declined to exercise jurisdiction on the ground that a court of Georgia is the more appropriate forum to determine the custody of the child under Code Section 19-9-67 or 19-9-68; or

(4) No court of any other state would have jurisdiction under the criteria specified in paragraph (1), (2), or (3) of this subsection.

-From Sections 19-9-61 and 19-9-41 of the Georgia Code.

Definitions.

Georgia law recognizes the following definitions of custody:

(1) 'Joint custody' means joint legal custody, joint physical custody, or both joint legal custody and joint physical custody. In making an order for joint custody, the court may order joint legal custody without ordering joint physical custody.

(2) 'Joint legal custody' means both parents have equal rights and responsibilities for major decisions concerning the child, including the child's education, health care, and religious training; provided, however, that the court may designate one parent to have sole power to make certain decisions while both parents retain equal rights and responsibilities for other decisions.

(3) 'Joint physical custody' means that physical custody is shared by the parents in such a way as to assure the child of substantially equal time and contact with both parents.

(4) 'Sole custody' means a person, including, but not limited to, a parent, has been awarded permanent custody of a child by a court order. Unless otherwise provided by court order, the person awarded sole custody of a child shall have the rights and responsibilities for major decisions concerning the child, including the child's education, health care, and religious training, and the noncustodial parent shall have the right to visitation. A person who has not been awarded custody of a child by court order shall not be considered as the sole legal custodian while exercising visitation rights.

-From Section 19-9-6 of the Georgia Code

Factors in Determining Custody.

In all cases in which the custody of any child is at issue between the parents, there shall be no prima-facie right to the custody of the child in the father or mother. There shall be no presumption in favor of any particular form of custody, legal or physical, nor in favor of either parent. Joint custody may be considered as an alternative form of custody by the judge and the judge at any temporary or permanent hearing may grant sole custody, joint custody, joint legal custody, or joint physical custody as appropriate.

The judge hearing the issue of custody shall make a determination of custody of a child and such matter shall not be decided by a jury. The judge may take into consideration all the circumstances of the case, including the improvement of the health of the party seeking a change in custody provisions, in determining to whom custody of the child should be awarded. The duty of the judge in all such cases shall be to exercise discretion to look to and determine solely what is for the best interest of the child and what will best promote the child's welfare and happiness and to make his or her award accordingly.

In determining the best interests of the child, the judge may consider any relevant factor including, but not limited to:

(A) The love, affection, bonding, and emotional ties existing between each parent and the child;

(B) The love, affection, bonding, and emotional ties existing between the child and his or her siblings, half siblings, and stepsiblings and the residence of such other children;

(C) The capacity and disposition of each parent to give the child love, affection, and guidance and to continue the education and rearing of the child;

(D) Each parent's knowledge and familiarity of the child and the child's needs;

(E) The capacity and disposition of each parent to provide the child with food, clothing, medical care, day-to-day needs, and other necessary basic care, with consideration made for the potential payment of child support by the other parent;

(F) The home environment of each parent considering the promotion of nurturance and safety of the child rather than superficial or material factors;

(G) The importance of continuity in the child's life and the length of time the child has lived in a stable, satisfactory environment and the desirability of maintaining continuity;

(H) The stability of the family unit of each of the parents and the presence or absence of each parent's support systems within the community to benefit the child;

(I) The mental and physical health of each parent;

(J) Each parent's involvement, or lack thereof, in the child's educational, social, and extracurricular activities;

(K) Each parent's employment schedule and the related flexibility or limitations, if any, of a parent to care for the child;

(L) The home, school, and community record and history of the child, as well as any health or educational special needs of the child;

(M) Each parent's past performance and relative abilities for future performance of parenting responsibilities;

(N) The willingness and ability of each of the parents to facilitate and encourage a close and continuing parent-child relationship between the child and the other parent, consistent with the best interest of the child;

(O) Any recommendation by a court appointed custody evaluator or guardian ad litem;

(P) Any evidence of family violence or sexual, mental, or physical child abuse or criminal history of either parent; and

(Q) Any evidence of substance abuse by either parent.

In all cases in which the child has reached the age of 14 years, the child shall have the right to select the parent with whom he or she desires to live. The child's selection shall be controlling, unless the parent so selected is determined not to be a fit and proper person to have the custody of the child.

In all cases in which the child has reached the age of at least 11 but not 14 years, the court shall consider the desires, if any, and educational needs of the child in determining which parent shall have custody. The court shall have complete discretion in making this determination, and the child's desires are not controlling. The court shall further have broad discretion as to how the child's desires are to be considered, including through the report of a guardian ad litem. The best interest of the child standard shall be controlling.

The desire of a child who has reached the age of 11 years but not 14 years shall not, in and of itself, constitute a material change of conditions or circumstances in any action seeking a modification or change in the custody of that child.

The court may issue an order granting temporary custody to the selected parent for a trial period not to exceed six months regarding the custody of a child who has reached the age of at least 11 years where the judge hearing the case determines such a temporary order is appropriate.

-From Section 19-9-3 of the Georgia Code.

Hawaii

In awarding child custody, the court shall be guided by the following guidelines:
(1) Custody should be awarded to either parent or to both parents according to the best interests of the child;
(2) Custody may be awarded to persons other than the father or mother whenever the award serves the best interest of the child. Any person who has had de facto custody of the child in a stable and wholesome home and is a fit and proper person shall be entitled prima facie to an award of custody;
(3) If a child is of sufficient age and capacity to reason, so as to form an intelligent preference, the child's wishes as to custody will be considered and be given due weight by the court;
(4) Whenever good cause appears, the court may require an investigation and report concerning the care, welfare, and custody of any minor child of the parties. When so directed by the court, investigators or professional personnel attached to or assisting the court shall make investigations and reports which shall be made available to all interested parties and counsel before hearing, and the reports may be received in evidence if no objection is made and, if objection is made, may be received in evidence provided the person or persons responsible for the report are available for cross-examination as to any matter that has been investigated;
(5) The court may hear the testimony of any person or expert produced by any party or upon the court's own motion, whose skill, insight, knowledge, or experience is such that the person's or expert's testimony is relevant to a just and reasonable determination of what is for the best physical, mental, moral, and spiritual well-being of the child whose custody is at issue;
(6) Any child custody award shall be subject to modification or change whenever the best interests of the child require or justify the modification or change and, wherever practicable, the same person who made the original order shall hear the motion or petition for modification of the prior award;

(7) Reasonable visitation rights shall be awarded to parents, grandparents, and any person interested in the welfare of the child in the discretion of the court, unless it is shown that rights of visitation are detrimental to the best interests of the child;

(8) The court may appoint a guardian ad litem to represent the interests of the child and may assess the reasonable fees and expenses of the guardian ad litem as costs of the action, payable in whole or in part by either or both parties as the circumstances may justify;

(9) In every proceeding where there is a dispute as to the custody of a child, a determination by the court that family violence has been committed by a parent raises a refutable presumption that it is detrimental to the child and not in the best interest of the child to be placed in sole custody, joint legal custody, or joint physical custody with the perpetrator of family violence. In addition to other factors that a court must consider in a proceeding in which the custody of a child or visitation by a parent is at issue, and in which the court has made a finding of family violence by a parent:

   (A) The court shall consider as primary the safety and well-being of the child and of the parent who is the victim of family violence;

   (B) The court shall consider the perpetrator's history of causing physical harm, bodily injury, assault, or causing reasonable fear of physical harm, bodily injury, or assault, to another person; and

   (C) If a parent is absent or relocates because of an act of family violence by the other parent, the absence or relocation shall not be a factor that weighs against the parent in determining custody or visitation;

(10) A court may award visitation to a parent who committed family violence only if the court finds that adequate provision for the physical safety and psychological well-being of the child and adequate provision for the safety of the parent who is a victim of family violence can be made.

Idaho

In a divorce, the court may award the custody, care and education of the children as may seem necessary or proper in the best interests of the children. The court should consider all relevant factors, which may include:

(a) The wishes of the child's parent or parents as to his or her custody;

(b) The wishes of the child as to his or her custodian;

(c) The interaction and interrelationship of the child with his or her parent or parents, and his or her siblings;

(d) The child's adjustment to his or her home, school, and community;

(e) The character and circumstances of all individuals involved;

(f) The need to promote continuity and stability in the life of the child; and

(g) Domestic violence, whether or not in the presence of the child.

-From 32-717 of the Idaho Statutes.

Access to Records.

Notwithstanding any other provisions of law, access to records and information pertaining to a minor child including, but not limited to, medical, dental, health, and school or educational records, shall not be denied to a parent because the parent is not the child's custodial parent.

However, information concerning the minor child's address shall be deleted from such records to a parent, if the custodial parent has advised the records custodian in writing to do so.

-From 32-717A of the Idaho Statutes.

Illinois
Illinois Laws on Best Interest of the Child.
(750 ILCS 5/602)
The court shall determine custody in accordance with the best interest of the child. The court shall consider all relevant factors including the following guidelines:
1. The wishes of the child's parent or parents as to custody of the child;
2. The wishes of the child as to custody;
3. The interaction and interrelationship of the child with his parent or parents, his siblings and any other person who may significantly affect the child's best interest;
4. The child's adjustment to his home, school and community;
5. The mental and physical health of all individuals involved;
6. The physical violence or threat of physical violence by the child's potential custodian, whether directed against the child or directed against another person;
7. The occurrence of ongoing abuse as defined in Section 103 of the Illinois Domestic Violence Act of 1986, whether directed against the child or directed against another person; and
8. The willingness and ability of each parent to facilitate and encourage a close and continuing relationship between the other parent and the child.

The court doesn't consider conduct of a present or proposed custodian that does not affect the relationship to the child.

Laws of Joint Custody.
(750 ILCS 5/602.1)
Unless the court finds the occurrence of ongoing abuse, it shall presume that the maximum involvement and cooperation of both parents regarding the physical, mental, moral, and emotional well-being of their child is in the best interest of the child. There shall be no presumption in favor of or against joint custody but upon the application of either or both parents, or upon its own motion, the court shall consider an award of joint custody. The court may enter an order of joint custody if it determines that joint custody would be in the best interests of the child, taking into account the following:
1. The ability of the parents to cooperate effectively and consistently in matters that directly affect the joint parenting of the child. "Ability of the parents to cooperate" means the parents' capacity to substantially comply with a Joint Parenting Order. The court shall not consider the inability of the parents to cooperate effectively and consistently in matters that do not directly affect the joint parenting of the child;

2. The residential circumstances of each parent; and

3. All other factors which may be relevant to the best interest of the child.

Access to Records.
Illinois laws require that neither parent shall be denied access to records and information pertaining to a child, including but not limited to medical, dental, child care and school records unless one parent is prohibited access to those records by a protective order.

Educational Program and Divorce.
In a case involving child custody, the court may order the parents to attend an educational program about the effects of divorce on children, if the court so desires.

Child Custody Guidelines.
The court shall determine custody and enter a custody order in accordance with the best interests of the child. In determining the best interests of the child, there is no presumption favoring either parent.

The court shall consider all relevant factors, including the following:

(1) The age and sex of the child.

(2) The wishes of the child's parent or parents.

(3) The wishes of the child, with more consideration given to the child's wishes if the child is at least 14 years of age.

(4) The interaction and interrelationship of the child with the child's parent or parents, the child's sibling, and any other person who may significantly affect the child's best interests.

(5) The child's adjustment to the child's home, school, and community.

(6) The mental and physical health of all individuals involved.

(7) Evidence of a pattern of domestic or family violence by either parent.

(8) Evidence that the child has been cared for by a de facto custodian.

-From 31-17-2-8 of the Indiana Code.

Joint Legal Custody Guidelines.
The court may award joint legal custody if it finds that to be in the best interest of the child. The court can award joint legal custody without awarding joint physical custody of the child. In determining whether an award of joint legal custody would be in the best interest of the child, the court shall consider it a matter of primary, but not determinative, importance that the persons awarded joint custody have agreed to an award of joint legal custody. The court shall also consider:

(1) the fitness and suitability of each of the persons awarded joint custody;

(2) whether the persons awarded joint custody are willing and able to communicate and cooperate in advancing the child's welfare;

(3) the wishes of the child, with more consideration given to the child's wishes if the child is at least 14 years of age; and

(4) whether the child has established a close and beneficial relationship with both of the persons awarded joint custody;

(5) whether the persons awarded joint custody live in close proximity to each other and plan to continue to do so; and

(6) the nature of the physical and emotional environment in the home of each of the persons awarded joint custody.

-From 31-17-2-13 through 15 of the Indiana Code.

Indiana
Child Custody Guidelines.

The court shall determine custody and enter a custody order in accordance with the best interests of the child. In determining the best interests of the child, there is no presumption favoring either parent. The court shall consider all relevant factors, including the following:

(1) The age and sex of the child.

(2) The wishes of the child's parent or parents.

(3) The wishes of the child, with more consideration given to the child's wishes if the child is at least 14 years of age.

(4) The interaction and interrelationship of the child with the child's parent or parents, the child's sibling, and any other person who may significantly affect the child's best interests.

(5) The child's adjustment to the child's home, school, and community.

(6) The mental and physical health of all individuals involved.

(7) Evidence of a pattern of domestic or family violence by either parent.

(8) Evidence that the child has been cared for by a de facto custodian.

-From 31-17-2-8 of the Indiana Code.

Joint Legal Custody Guidelines.

The court may award joint legal custody if it finds that to be in the best interest of the child. The court can award joint legal custody without awarding joint physical custody of the child. In determining whether an award of joint legal custody would be in the best interest of the child, the court shall consider it a matter of primary, but not determinative, importance that the persons awarded joint custody have agreed to an award of joint legal custody. The court shall also consider:

(1) the fitness and suitability of each of the persons awarded joint custody;

(2) whether the persons awarded joint custody are willing and able to communicate and cooperate in advancing the child's welfare;

(3) the wishes of the child, with more consideration given to the child's wishes if the child is at least 14 years of age; and

(4) whether the child has established a close and beneficial relationship with both of the persons awarded joint custody;

(5) whether the persons awarded joint custody live in close proximity to each other and plan to continue to do so; and

(6) the nature of the physical and emotional environment in the home of each of the persons awarded joint custody.

-From 31-17-2-13 through 15 of the Indiana Code.

Iowa
Definitions.
"Joint custody" or "joint legal custody" means an award of legal custody of a minor child to both parents jointly under which both parents have legal custodial rights and responsibilities toward the child and under which neither parent has legal custodial rights superior to those of the other parent. Rights and responsibilities of joint legal custody include, but are not limited to, equal participation in decisions affecting the child's legal status, medical care, education, extracurricular activities, and religious instruction.

"Joint physical care" means an award of physical care of a minor child to both joint legal custodial parents under which both parents have rights and responsibilities toward the child including, but not limited to, shared parenting time with the child, maintaining homes for the child, providing routine care for the child and under which neither parent has physical care rights superior to those of the other parent.

"Legal custody" or "custody" means an award of the rights of legal custody of a minor child to a parent under which a parent has legal custodial rights and responsibilities toward the child. Rights and responsibilities of legal custody include, but are not limited to, decision making affecting the child's legal status, medical care, education, extracurricular activities, and religious instruction.

"Physical care" means the right and responsibility to maintain a home for the minor child and provide for the routine care of the child. Physical care awarded to one parent does not affect the other parent's rights and responsibilities as a joint legal custodian of the child.

-From Section 598.1 of the Iowa Code.

Parenting Course.
Iowa law requires that parties to any action which involves the issues of child custody or visitation must attend a court-approved course to "educate and sensitize the parties to the needs of any child or party during and subsequent to the proceeding". In all judicial districts, there are courses such as "Children in the Middle" or "Children Cope with Divorce". These classes are designed to help minimize the negative impact of divorce on children and educate parents about the needs of children whose parents are divorcing. Parents are required to attend within 45 days of the service of original notice or application for modification of an order.

-From Section 598.15 of the Iowa Code

Access to Records.
Unless otherwise ordered by the court in the custody decree, both parents shall have legal access to information concerning the child, including but not limited to medical, educational and law enforcement records.

-From Section 598.41 of the Iowa Code.

Custody of children.
The court, insofar as is reasonable and in the best interest of the child, shall order the

custody award, including liberal visitation rights where appropriate, which will assure the child the opportunity for the maximum continuing physical and emotional contact with both parents after the parents have separated or dissolved the marriage, and which will encourage parents to share the rights and responsibilities of raising the child unless direct physical harm or significant emotional harm to the child, other children, or a parent is likely to result from such contact with one parent.

If the court finds that a history of domestic abuse exists, a rebuttable presumption against the awarding of joint custody exists.

The court shall consider the denial by one parent of the child's opportunity for maximum continuing contact with the other parent, without just cause, a significant factor in determining the proper custody arrangement.

-From Section 598.41 of the Iowa Code.

Factors Used in Determining Custody of Minor Child.
In considering what custody arrangement is in the best interest of the minor child, the court shall consider the following factors:
a. Whether each parent would be a suitable custodian for the child.
b. Whether the psychological and emotional needs and development of the child will suffer due to lack of active contact with and attention from both parents.
c. Whether the parents can communicate with each other regarding the child's needs.
d. Whether both parents have actively cared for the child before and since the separation.
e. Whether each parent can support the other parent's relationship with the child.
f. Whether the custody arrangement is in accord with the child's wishes or whether the child has strong opposition, taking into consideration the child's age and maturity.
g. Whether one or both the parents agree or are opposed to joint custody.
h. The geographic proximity of the parents.
i. Whether the safety of the child, other children, or the other parent will be jeopardized by the awarding of joint custody or by unsupervised or unrestricted visitation.
j. Whether a history of domestic abuse, as defined in section 236.2 , exists. In determining whether a history of domestic abuse exists, the court's consideration shall include, but is not limited to, commencement of an action pursuant to section 236.3 , the issuance of a protective order against the parent or the issuance of a court order or consent agreement pursuant to section 236.5 , the issuance of an emergency order pursuant to section 236.6 , the holding of a parent in contempt pursuant to section 236.8 , the response of a peace officer to the scene of alleged domestic abuse or the arrest of a parent following response to a report of alleged domestic abuse, or a conviction for domestic abuse assault pursuant to section 708.2A .

-From Section 598.41 of the Iowa Code.

Kansas
(60-1610)(a)(3)
If the parties have entered into a parenting plan it shall be presumed that the agreement is in the best interest of the child, unless specific findings prove otherwise. The court shall determine custody of a child in accordance with the best interests of the child, considering the following factors, among others:
1. The length of time that the child has been under the actual care and control of any person other than a parent and the circumstances relating thereto;
2. The desires of the child's parents as to custody or residency;
3. The desires of the child as to the child's custody or residency;
4. The interaction and interrelationship of the child with parents, siblings and any other person who may significantly affect the child's best interests;
5. The child's adjustment to the child's home, school and community;
6. The willingness and ability of each parent to respect and appreciate the bond between the child and the other parent and to allow for a continuing relationship between the child and the other parent; and
7. Evidence of spousal abuse.

The court shows a preference for joint legal custody over sole legal custody in (60-1610)(a)(4)

Kentucky
Guidelines Used by the Court to Determine Child Custody.
The court shall determine custody in accordance with the best interests of the child, and equal consideration shall be given to each parent. The court shall consider all relevant factors including:
(a) The wishes of the child's parent or parents, and any de facto custodian, as to his custody;
(b) The wishes of the child as to his custodian;
(c) The interaction and interrelationship of the child with his parent or parents, his siblings, and any other person who may significantly affect the child's best interests;
(d) The child's adjustment to his home, school, and community;
(e) The mental and physical health of all individuals involved;
(f) Information, records, and evidence of domestic violence as defined in KRS 403.720;
(g) The extent to which the child has been cared for, nurtured, and supported by any de facto custodian;
(h) The intent of the parent or parents in placing the child with a de facto custodian; and
(i) The circumstances under which the child was placed or allowed to remain in the custody of a de facto custodian, including whether the parent now seeking custody was previously prevented from doing so as a result of domestic violence as defined in KRS 403.720 and whether the child was placed with a de facto custodian to allow the parent now seeking custody to seek employment, work, or attend school.

The court shall not consider conduct of a proposed custodian that does not affect his relationship to the child. If domestic violence and abuse is alleged, the court shall determine the extent to which the domestic violence and abuse has affected the child and the child's relationship to both parents.

The abandonment of the family residence by a custodial party shall not be considered where said party was physically harmed or was seriously threatened with physical harm by his or her spouse, when such harm or threat of harm was causally related to the abandonment.

-From Section 403.270 of the Kentucky Statutes.

Visitation with Minor Child.
A parent not granted custody of the child is entitled to reasonable visitation rights unless the court finds, after a hearing, that visitation would endanger seriously the child's physical, mental, moral, or emotional health. Upon request of either party, the court shall issue orders which are specific as to the frequency, timing, duration, conditions, and method of scheduling visitation and which reflect the development age of the child.

If domestic violence and abuse, as defined in KRS 403.720, has been alleged, the court shall, after a hearing, determine the visitation arrangement, if any, which would not endanger seriously the child's or the custodial parent's physical, mental, or emotional health.

-From Section 403.320 of the Kentucky Statutes.

Custodian of the Minor Child.
Except as otherwise agreed by the parties in writing at the time of the custody decree, the custodian may determine the child's upbringing, including his education, health care, and religious training, unless the court after hearing, finds, upon motion by the noncustodial parent, that in the absence of a specific limitation of the custodian's authority, the child's physical health would be endangered or his emotional development significantly impaired.
-From Section 403.330 of the Kentucky Statutes.

Louisiana

Art. 131. Court to determine custody

In a proceeding for divorce or thereafter, the court shall award custody of a child in accordance with the best interest of the child.

Maine
Shared Legal Custody and Maine Laws.
When the parents have agreed to share parental rights and responsibilities, the court will make that award unless there is substantial evidence that it should not be ordered. (1653)(2)(A)

Maine Laws on Best Interest of the Child.
The court shall consider the best interest of the child in making an award for custody. The safety and well-being of the child are primary concerns, taking into account the following factors:
1. The age of the child;
2. The relationship of the child with the child's parents and any other persons who may significantly affect the child's welfare;
3. The preference of the child, if old enough to express a meaningful preference;
4. The duration and adequacy of the child's current living arrangements and the desirability of maintaining continuity;
5. The stability of any proposed living arrangements for the child;
6. The motivation of the parties involved and their capacities to give the child love, affection and guidance;
7. The child's adjustment to the child's present home, school and community;
8. The capacity of each parent to allow and encourage frequent and continuing contact between the child and the other parent, including physical access;
9. The capacity of each parent to cooperate or to learn to cooperate in child care;
10. Methods for assisting parental cooperation and resolving disputes and each parent's willingness to use those methods;
11. The effect on the child if one parent has sole authority over the child's upbringing;
12. The existence of domestic abuse between the parents, in the past or currently, and how that abuse affects the child's safety and emotional health;
13. The existence of any history of child abuse by a parent;
14. All other factors having a reasonable bearing on the physical and psychological well-being of the child;
15. A parent's prior willful misuse of the protection from abuse process in chapter 101 in order to gain tactical advantage in a proceeding involving the determination of parental rights and responsibilities of a minor child. Such willful misuse may only be considered if established by clear and convincing evidence, and if it is further found by clear and convincing evidence that in the particular circumstances of the parents and child, that willful misuse tends to show that the acting parent will in the future have a lessened ability and willingness to cooperate and work with the other parent in their shared responsibilities for the child. The court shall articulate findings of fact whenever relying upon this factor as part of its determination of a child's best interest. The voluntary dismissal of a protection from abuse petition may not, taken alone, be treated as evidence of the willful misuse of the protection from abuse process; and
16. If the child is under one year of age, whether the child is being breast-fed.

Maryland
Maryland law lists no specific guidelines or factors the court uses to determine child custody. If there has been abuse or child neglect, the court might deny custody or visitation to the parent who committed the offense.

Unless otherwise ordered by a court, the law prohibits access to medical, dental, and educational records concerning the child from being denied to a parent because the parent does not have physical custody of the child. (9-104)

Massachusetts
Definitions.
For the purposes of this section, the following words shall have the following meaning unless the context requires otherwise:

"Sole legal custody", one parent shall have the right and responsibility to make major decisions regarding the child's welfare including matters of education, medical care and emotional, moral and religious development.

"Shared legal custody", continued mutual responsibility and involvement by both parents in major decisions regarding the child's welfare including matters of education, medical care and emotional, moral and religious development.

"Sole physical custody", a child shall reside with and be under the supervision of one parent, subject to reasonable visitation by the other parent, unless the court determines that such visitation would not be in the best interest of the child.

"Shared physical custody", a child shall have periods of residing with and being under the supervision of each parent; provided, however, that physical custody shall be shared by the parents in such a way as to assure a child frequent and continued contact with both parents.

-From Section 208:31 of the General Laws of Massachusetts.

Custody Guidelines.
Where the parents have reached an agreement providing for the custody of the children, the court may enter an order in accordance with such agreement, unless specific findings are made by the court indicating that such an order would not be in the best interests of the children.

In making an order or judgment relative to the custody of children, the rights of the parents shall, in the absence of misconduct, be held to be equal, and the happiness and welfare of the children shall determine their custody. When considering the happiness and welfare of the child, the court shall consider whether or not the child's present or past living conditions adversely affect his physical, mental, moral or emotional health.

-From Section 208:31 of the General Laws of Massachusetts.

Access to Records.
Unless otherwise ordered, the entry of a custody order shall not negate or impede the ability of the non-custodial parent to have access to the academic, medical, hospital or other health records of the child.

-From Section 208:31 of the General Laws of Massachusetts.

Education Program for Divorcing Parents.
All parties to a divorce action in which there are minor children must attend and participate in an approved Parent Education Program. Parties must register with an approved provider within 60 days of service of the complaint and attend the next available session.

-From Standing Order 103

Michigan
Best Interests of the Child.
Parenting time shall be granted in accordance with the best interests of the child. "Best interests of the child" means the sum total of the following factors to be considered, evaluated, and determined by the court:
(a) The love, affection, and other emotional ties existing between the parties involved and the child.
(b) The capacity and disposition of the parties involved to give the child love, affection, and guidance and to continue the education and raising of the child in his or her religion or creed, if any.
(c) The capacity and disposition of the parties involved to provide the child with food, clothing, medical care or other remedial care recognized and permitted under the laws of this state in place of medical care, and other material needs.
(d) The length of time the child has lived in a stable, satisfactory environment, and the desirability of maintaining continuity.
(e) The permanence, as a family unit, of the existing or proposed custodial home or homes.
(f) The moral fitness of the parties involved.
(g) The mental and physical health of the parties involved.
(h) The home, school, and community record of the child.
(i) The reasonable preference of the child, if the court considers the child to be of sufficient age to express preference.
(j) The willingness and ability of each of the parties to facilitate and encourage a close and continuing parent-child relationship between the child and the other parent or the child and the parents.
(k) Domestic violence, regardless of whether the violence was directed against or witnessed by the child.
(l) Any other factor considered by the court to be relevant to a particular child custody dispute.

-From Section 722.23 of the Michigan Revised Statutes

Factors in Determining Visitation.
Michigan refers to visitation as "parenting time". According to Michigan statutes, the court may consider the following factors when determining the frequency, duration, and type of parenting time to be granted:
(a) The existence of any special circumstances or needs of the child.
(b) Whether the child is a nursing child less than 6 months of age, or less than 1 year of age if the child receives substantial nutrition through nursing.
(c) The reasonable likelihood of abuse or neglect of the child during parenting time.

(d) The reasonable likelihood of abuse of a parent resulting from the exercise of parenting time.

(e) The inconvenience to, and burdensome impact or effect on, the child of traveling for purposes of parenting time.

(f) Whether a parent can reasonably be expected to exercise parenting time in accordance with the court order.

(g) Whether a parent has frequently failed to exercise reasonable parenting time.

(h) The threatened or actual detention of the child with the intent to retain or conceal the child from the other parent or from a third person who has legal custody. A custodial parent's temporary residence with the child in a domestic violence shelter shall not be construed as evidence of the custodial parent's intent to retain or conceal the child from the other parent.

(i) Any other relevant factors.

During the time a child is with a parent to whom parenting time has been awarded, that parent shall decide all routine matters concerning the child.

-From Section 722.27b of the Michigan Revised Statutes

Agreement by the Parents.

If the parents of a child agree on parenting time terms, the court shall order the parenting time terms unless the court determines on the record by clear and convincing evidence that the parenting time terms are not in the best interests of the child.

-From Section 722.27b of the Michigan Revised Statutes

Joint Custody.

"Joint custody" means (a) that the child shall reside alternately for specific periods with each of the parents, and (b) that the parents shall share decision-making authority as to the important decisions affecting the welfare of the child.

The court shall determine whether joint custody is in the best interest of the child by considering the following factors:

(a) The factors listed above for "Best Interests of the Child".

(b) Whether the parents will be able to cooperate and generally agree concerning important decisions affecting the welfare of the child.

If the parents agree on joint custody, the court shall award joint custody unless the court determines on the record, based upon clear and convincing evidence, that joint custody is not in the best interests of the child.

Joint custody shall not eliminate the responsibility for child support.

Each parent shall be responsible for child support based on the needs of the child and the actual resources of each parent. An order of joint custody, in and of itself, shall not constitute grounds for modifying a support order.

-From Section 722.26a of the Michigan Revised Statutes

Access to Records.
Notwithstanding any other provision of law, a parent shall not be denied access to records or information concerning his or her child because the parent is not the child's custodial parent, unless the parent is prohibited from having access to the records or information by a protective order. "Records or information" includes, but is not limited to, medical, dental, and school records, day care provider's records, and notification of meetings regarding the child's education.
-From Section 722.30 of the Michigan Revised Statutes

Minnesota
Minnesota Laws on Best Interest of the Child.
(518.17)
Minnesota laws assign custody based on the "best interests of the child," meaning all relevant factors to be considered and evaluated by the court including:
1. The wishes of the child's parent or parents as to custody;
2. The reasonable preference of the child as to custody, if the court deems the child to be of sufficient age to express preference;
3. The child's primary caretaker;
4. The intimacy of the relationship between each parent and the child;
5. The interaction and interrelationship of the child with a parent or parents, siblings, and any other person who may significantly affect the child's best interests;
6. The child's adjustment to home, school, and community;
7. The length of time the child has lived in a stable, satisfactory environment and the desirability of maintaining continuity;
8. The permanence, as a family unit, of the existing or proposed custodial home;
9. The mental and physical health of all individuals involved; except that a disability of a proposed custodian or the child shall not be determinative of the custody of the child, unless the proposed custody arrangement is not in the best interest of the child;
10. The capacity and disposition of the parties to give the child love, affection, and guidance, and to continue educating and raising the child in the child's culture and religion or creed, if any;
11. The child's cultural background;
12. The effect on the child of the actions of an abuser, if related to domestic abuse that has occurred between the parents or between a parent and another individual, whether or not the individual alleged to have committed domestic abuse is or ever was a family or household member of the parent; and
13. The disposition of each parent to encourage and permit frequent and continuing contact by the other parent with the child.

The court may not use one factor to the exclusion of all others in determining custody of a child. Minnesota laws do not allow the court to consider conduct of a proposed custodian that does not affect the custodian's relationship to the child.

Joint Legal or Physical Custody Guidelines.
In addition to the factors listed above, where either joint legal custody or joint

physical custody is contemplated or sought, the court shall consider the following relevant factors:

1. The ability of parents to cooperate in the rearing of their children;
2. Methods for resolving disputes regarding any major decision concerning the life of the child, and the parents' willingness to use those methods;
3. Whether it would be detrimental to the child if one parent were to have sole authority over the child's upbringing; and
4. Whether domestic abuse has occurred between the parties.

Joint Legal Custody.
The court shall use a refutable presumption that upon request of either or both parties, joint legal custody is in the best interest of the child.

However, the court shall use a refutable presumption that joint legal or physical custody is not in the best interests of the child if domestic abuse has occurred between the parents.

Access to Records.
Minnesota laws give each party the right of access to, and to receive copies of, school, medical, dental, religious training, and other important records and information about the minor children. The laws also give each party the right of access to information regarding health or dental insurance available to the minor children. Each party shall keep the other party informed as to the name and address of the school of attendance of the minor children. Each party has the right to be informed by school officials about the children's welfare, educational progress and status, and to attend school and parent-teacher conferences. The school is not required to hold a separate conference for each party. In case of an accident or serious illness of a minor child, each party shall notify the other party of the accident or illness, and the name of the health care provider and the place of treatment. Each party has the right to reasonable access and telephone contact with the minor children. The court may waive any of the rights under this section if it finds it is necessary to protect the welfare of a party or child.

Mississippi
§ 93-5-24. Types of custody awarded by court; joint custody; no presumption in favor of maternal custody; access to information pertaining to child by noncustodial parent; restrictions on custody by parent with history of perpetrating family violence; rebuttable presumption that such custody is not in the best interest of the child; factors in reaching determinations; visitation orders.

(1) Custody shall be awarded as follows according to the best interests of the child:
    (a) Physical and legal custody to both parents jointly pursuant to subsections (2) through (7).
    (b) Physical custody to both parents jointly pursuant to subsections (2) through (7) and legal custody to either parent.

(c) Legal custody to both parents jointly pursuant to subsections (2) through (7) and physical custody to either parent.

(d) Physical and legal custody to either parent.

(e) Upon a finding by the court that both of the parents of the child have abandoned or deserted such child or that both such parents are mentally, morally or otherwise unfit to rear and train the child the court may award physical and legal custody to:

(i) The person in whose home the child has been living in a wholesome and stable environment; or

(ii) Physical and legal custody to any other person deemed by the court to be suitable and able to provide adequate and proper care and guidance for the child.

In making an order for custody to either parent or to both parents jointly, the court, in its discretion, may require the parents to submit to the court a plan for the implementation of the custody order.

(2) Joint custody may be awarded where irreconcilable differences is the ground for divorce, in the discretion of the court, upon application of both parents.

(3) In other cases, joint custody may be awarded, in the discretion of the court, upon application of one or both parents.

(4) There shall be a presumption that joint custody is in the best interest of a minor child where both parents have agreed to an award of joint custody.

(5) (a) For the purposes of this section, "joint custody" means joint physical and legal custody.

(b) For the purposes of this section, "physical custody" means those periods of time in which a child resides with or is under the care and supervision of one (1) of the parents.

(c) For the purposes of this section, "joint physical custody" means that each of the parents shall have significant periods of physical custody. Joint physical custody shall be shared by the parents in such a way so as to assure a child of frequent and continuing contact with both parents.

(d) For the purposes of this section, "legal custody" means the decision-making rights, the responsibilities and the authority relating to the health, education and welfare of a child.

(e) For the purposes of this section, "joint legal custody" means that the parents or parties share the decision-making rights, the responsibilities and the authority relating to the health, education and welfare of a child.

An award of joint legal custody obligates the parties to exchange information concerning the health, education and welfare of the minor child, and to confer with one another in the exercise of decision-making rights, responsibilities and authority.

An award of joint physical and legal custody obligates the parties to exchange information concerning the health, education and welfare of the minor child, and unless allocated, apportioned or decreed, the parents or parties shall confer with one another in the exercise of decision-making rights, responsibilities and authority.

(6) Any order for joint custody may be modified or terminated upon the petition of both parents or upon the petition of one (1) parent showing that a material change in circumstances has occurred.

(7) There shall be no presumption that it is in the best interest of a child that a mother be awarded either legal or physical custody.

(8) Notwithstanding any other provision of law, access to records and information pertaining to a minor child, including, but not limited to, medical, dental and school records, shall not be denied to a parent because the parent is not the child's custodial parent.

(9) (a)

(i) In every proceeding where the custody of a child is in dispute, there shall be a rebuttable presumption that it is detrimental to the child and not in the best interest of the child to be placed in sole custody, joint legal custody or joint physical custody of a parent who has a history of perpetrating family violence. The court may find a history of perpetrating family violence if the court finds, by a preponderance of the evidence, one (1) incident of family violence that has resulted in serious bodily injury to, or a pattern of family violence against, the party making the allegation or a family household member of either party. The court shall make written findings to document how and why the presumption was or was not triggered.

(ii) This presumption may only be rebutted by a preponderance of the evidence.

(iii) In determining whether the presumption set forth in subsection (9) has been overcome, the court shall consider all of the following factors:

1. Whether the perpetrator of family violence has demonstrated that giving sole or joint physical or legal custody of a child to the perpetrator is in the best interest of the child because of the other parent's absence, mental illness, substance abuse or such other circumstances which affect the best interest of the child or children;

2. Whether the perpetrator has successfully completed a batterer's treatment program;

3. Whether the perpetrator has successfully completed a program of alcohol or drug abuse counseling if the court determines that counseling is appropriate;

4. Whether the perpetrator has successfully completed a parenting class if the court determines the class to be appropriate;

5. If the perpetrator is on probation or parole, whether he or she is restrained by a protective order granted after a hearing, and whether he or she has complied with its terms and conditions; and

6. Whether the perpetrator of domestic violence has committed any further acts of domestic violence.

(iv) The court shall make written findings to document how and why the presumption was or was not rebutted.

(b)

(i) If custody is awarded to a suitable third person, it shall not be until the natural grandparents of the child have been excluded and such person shall not allow access to a violent parent except as ordered by the court.

(ii) If the court finds that both parents have a history of perpetrating family violence, but the court finds that parental custody would be in the best interest of the child, custody may be awarded solely to the parent less likely to continue to perpetrate family violence. In such a case, the court may mandate completion of a treatment program by the custodial parent.

(c) If the court finds that the allegations of domestic violence are completely unfounded, the chancery court shall order the alleging party to pay all court costs and reasonable attorney's fees incurred by the defending party in responding to such allegations.

(d)

(i) A court may award visitation by a parent who committed domestic or family violence only if the court finds that adequate provision for the safety of the child and the parent who is a victim of domestic or family violence can be made.

(ii) In a visitation order, a court may take any of the following actions:

1. Order an exchange of the child to occur in a protected setting;

2. Order visitation supervised in a manner to be determined by the court;

3. Order the perpetrator of domestic or family violence to attend and complete to the satisfaction of the court a program of intervention for perpetrators or other designated counseling as a condition of visitation;

4. Order the perpetrator of domestic or family violence to abstain from possession or consumption of alcohol or controlled substances during the visitation and for twenty-four (24) hours preceding the visitation;

5. Order the perpetrator of domestic or family violence to pay a fee to defray the cost of supervised visitation;

6. Prohibit overnight visitation;

7. Require a bond from the perpetrator of domestic or family violence for the return and safety of the child; or

8. Impose any other condition that is deemed necessary to provide for the safety of the child, the victim of family or domestic violence, or other family or household member.

(iii) Whether or not visitation is allowed, the court may order the address of the child or the victim of family or domestic violence to be kept confidential.

(e) The court may refer but shall not order an adult who is a victim of family or domestic violence to attend counseling relating to the victim's status or behavior as a victim, individually or with the perpetrator of domestic or family violence, as a condition of receiving custody of a child or as a condition of visitation.

(f) If a court allows a family or household member to supervise visitation, the court shall establish conditions to be followed during visitation.

> 1983, ch. 513, §§ 1, 2; Laws, 2000, ch. 453, § 1; Laws, 2003, ch. 475, § 1,
> eff from and after July 1, 2003.

Missouri
Definitions.
As used in this chapter, unless the context clearly indicates otherwise:

(1) "Custody" means joint legal custody, sole legal custody, joint physical custody or sole physical custody or any combination thereof.

(2) "Joint legal custody" means that the parents share the decision-making rights, responsibilities, and authority relating to the health, education and welfare of the child, and, unless allocated, apportioned, or decreed, the parents shall confer

with one another in the exercise of decision-making rights, responsibilities, and authority.

(3) "Joint physical custody" means an order awarding each of the parents significant, but not necessarily equal, periods of time during which a child resides with or is under the care and supervision of each of the parents. Joint physical custody shall be shared by the parents in such a way as to assure the child of frequent, continuing and meaningful contact with both parents.

-From Section 452.375 of the Missouri Revised Statutes.

Legal Custodian.

Except as otherwise ordered by the court or agreed by the parties in writing at the time of the custody decree, the legal custodian may determine the child's upbringing, including his education, health care, and religious training, unless the court after hearing finds, upon motion by the parent without legal custody, that in the absence of a specific limitation of the legal custodian's authority the child's physical health would be endangered or his emotional development impaired.

The legal custodian shall not exercise legal custody in such a way as to significantly and detrimentally impact the other parent's visitation or custody rights.

-From Section 452.405 of the Missouri Revised Statutes.

Best Interests of the Child, Custody Guidelines.

The general assembly finds and declares that it is the public policy of this state that frequent, continuing and meaningful contact with both parents after the parents have separated or dissolved their marriage is in the best interest of the child, except for cases where the court specifically finds that such contact is not in the best interest of the child, and that it is the public policy of this state to encourage parents to partici-pate in decisions affecting the health, education and welfare of their children, and to resolve disputes involving their children amicably through alternative dispute resolution. In order to effectuate these policies, the court shall determine the custody arrangement which will best assure both parents participate in such decisions and have frequent, continuing and meaningful contact with their children so long as it is in the best interests of the child.

The court shall determine custody in accordance with the best interests of the child. The court shall consider all relevant factors including:

(1) The wishes of the child's parents as to custody and the proposed parenting plan submitted by both parties;

(2) The needs of the child for a frequent, continuing and meaningful relationship with both parents and the ability and willingness of parents to actively perform their functions as mother and father for the needs of the child;

(3) The interaction and interrelationship of the child with parents, siblings, and any other person who may significantly affect the child's best interests;

(4) Which parent is more likely to allow the child frequent, continuing and meaning-ful contact with the other parent;

(5) The child's adjustment to the child's home, school, and community;

(6) The mental and physical health of all individuals involved, including any history of abuse of any individuals involved. If the court finds that a pattern of domestic

violence has occurred, and, if the court also finds that awarding custody to the abusive parent is in the best interest of the child, then the court shall enter written findings of fact and conclusions of law. Custody and visitation rights shall be ordered in a manner that best protects the child and any other child or children for whom the parent has custodial or visitation rights, and the parent or other family or household member who is the victim of domestic violence from any further harm;

(7) The intention of either parent to relocate the principal residence of the child; and

(8) The wishes of a child as to the child's custodian.

The fact that a parent sends his or her child or children to a home school, as defined in section 167.031, RSMo, shall not be the sole factor that a court considers in determining custody of such child or children.

-From Section 452.375 of the Missouri Revised Statutes.

Child's Wishes as to Custodian.
The court may interview the child in chambers to ascertain the child's wishes as to his custodian and relevant matters within his knowledge.

The court shall permit counsel to be present at the interview and to participate therein. The court shall cause a record of the interview to be made and to be made part of the record in the case.

-From Section 452.385 of the Missouri Revised Statutes.

Access to Records.
Unless a parent has been denied custody rights or visitation rights, both parents shall have access to records and information pertaining to a minor child, including, but not limited to, medical, dental, and school records. If the parent without custody has been granted restricted or supervised visitation because the court has found that the parent with custody or any child has been the victim of domestic violence by the parent without custody, the court may order that the reports and records made available pursuant to this subsection not include the address of the parent with custody or the child.

-From Section 452.375 of the Missouri Revised Statutes.

Relocation of Minor Child.
Notice of a proposed relocation of the residence of the child, or any party entitled to custody or visitation of the child, shall be given in writing by certified mail, return receipt requested, to any party with custody or visitation rights. Absent exigent circumstances as determined by a court with jurisdiction, written notice shall be provided at least 60 days in advance of the proposed relocation. The notice of the proposed relocation shall include the following information:

(1) The intended new residence, including the specific address and mailing address, if known, and if not known, the city;

(2) The home telephone number of the new residence, if known;

(3) The date of the intended move or proposed relocation;

(4) A brief statement of the specific reasons for the proposed relocation of a child, if applicable; and

(5) A proposal for a revised schedule of custody or visitation with the child, if applicable.

A party required to give notice of a proposed relocation has a continuing duty to provide a change in or addition to the above information as soon as such information becomes known.

In exceptional circumstances where the court makes a finding that the health or safety of any adult or child would be unreasonably placed at risk by the disclosure of the required identifying information concerning a proposed relocation of the child, the court may order that:

(1) The specific residence address and telephone number of the child, parent or person, and other identifying information shall not be disclosed in the pleadings, notice, other documents filed in the proceeding or the final order except for an in camera disclosure;

(2) The notice requirements provided by this section shall be waived to the extent necessary to protect the health or safety of a child or any adult; or

(3) Any other remedial action the court considers necessary to facilitate the legitimate needs of the parties and the best interest of the child.

The court shall consider a failure to provide notice of a proposed relocation of a child as:

(1) A factor in determining whether custody and visitation should be modified;

(2) A basis for ordering the return of the child if the relocation occurs without notice; and

(3) Sufficient cause to order the party seeking to relocate the child to pay reasonable expenses and attorneys fees incurred by the party objecting to the relocation.

The party seeking to relocate shall have the burden of proving that the proposed relocation is made in good faith and is in the best interest of the child.

-From Section 452.377 of the Missouri Revised Statutes.

Withholding Visitation.
If a party fails to comply with a provision of a decree or temporary order or injunction, the obligation of the other party to make payments for support or maintenance or to permit visitation is not suspended but he may move the court to grant an appropriate order.

A court with jurisdiction may abate, in whole or in part, any past or future obligation of support and may transfer the physical and legal or physical or legal custody of one or more children if it finds that a parent has, without good cause, failed to provide visitation or physical and legal or physical or legal custody to the other parent pursuant to the terms of a judgment of dissolution, legal separation or modifications thereof.

-From Sections 452.340 and 452.365 of the Missouri Revised Statutes.

Jurisdiction Over Children.

In order for a court to decide custody of your children, whether by agreement of the spouses or by decision of the court, that court must have jurisdiction. In order to have jurisdiction, one of the following must apply:

(a) The state of Missouri is the home state of the child at the time of commencement of the proceeding, or the state of Missouri was the child's home state within six months before commencement of the proceeding and the child is absent from this state for any reason, and a parent or person acting as parent continues to live in the state of Missouri.

"Home state" means the state in which, immediately preceding the filing of custody proceeding, the child lived with his parents, a parent, an institution; or a person acting as parent, for at least six consecutive months; or, in the case of a child less than six months old, the state in which the child lived from birth with any of the persons mentioned. Periods of temporary absence of any of the named persons are counted as part of the six-month or other period.

(b) It is in the best interest of the child that a court of the state of Missouri assume jurisdiction because:
    (i) The child and his parents, or the child and at least one litigant, have a significant connection with the state of Missouri; and
    (ii) There is available in the state of Missouri substantial evidence concerning the child's present or future care, protection, training, and personal relationships; or

(c) The child is physically present in the state of Missouri and:
    (i) The child has been abandoned; or
    (i) It is necessary in an emergency to protect the child because he has been subjected to or threatened with mistreatment or abuse, or is otherwise being neglected; or

(d) It appears that no other state would have jurisdiction, or another state has declined to exercise jurisdiction on the ground that the state of Missouri is the more appropriate forum to determine the custody of the child, and it is in the best interest of the child that Missouri assume jurisdiction. .

        -From Sections 452.445 and 452.450 of the Missouri Revised Statutes.

Montana
Child Custody Guidelines.

Montana laws use guidelines to determine custody in accordance with the best interest of the child. The court shall consider all relevant factors, which may include but are not limited to:

(a) the wishes of the child's parent or parents;
(b) the wishes of the child;
(c) the interaction and interrelationship of the child with the child's parent or parents and siblings and with any other person who significantly affects the child's best interest;
(d) the child's adjustment to home, school, and community;
(e) the mental and physical health of all individuals involved;
(f) physical abuse or threat of physical abuse by one parent against the other parent or the child;

(g) chemical dependency or chemical abuse on the part of either parent;

(h) continuity and stability of care;

(i) developmental needs of the child;

(j) whether a parent has knowingly failed to pay birth-related costs that the parent is able to pay, which is considered to be not in the child's best interests;

(k) whether a parent has knowingly failed to financially support a child that the parent is able to support, which is considered to be not in the child's best interests;

(l) whether the child has frequent and continuing contact with both parents, which is considered to be in the child's best interests unless the court determines, after a hearing, that contact with a parent would be detrimental to the child's best interests. In making that determination, the court shall consider evidence of physical abuse or threat of physical abuse by one parent against the other parent or the child.

(m) adverse effects on the child resulting from continuous and vexatious parenting plan amendment actions.

-From 40-4-212 of the Montana Code.

Moving with the Child.

A parent who intends to change residence must provide written notice to the other parent. If a parent's change in residence will significantly affect the child's contact with the other parent, notice must be served personally or given by certified mail not less than 30 days before the proposed change in residence, and must include a proposed revised residential schedule. Proof of service must be filed with the court that adopted the parenting plan. Failure of the parent who receives notice to respond to the written notice or to seek amendment of the residential schedule within the 30-day period constitutes acceptance of the proposed revised residential schedule.

-From 40-4-217 of the Montana Code.

Access to Records.

Notwithstanding any other provision of law, access to records and information pertaining to a minor child, including but not limited to medical, dental, law enforcement, and school records, may not be denied to a parent who is a party to a parenting plan.

-From 40-4-225 of the Montana Code.

Parenting Plan.

A parenting plan must be submitted to the court, including the allocation of parenting functions. "Parenting functions" means those aspects of the parent-child relationship in which the parent makes decisions and performs functions necessary for the care and growth of the child, which may include:

(a) maintaining a loving, stable, consistent, and nurturing relationship with the child;

(b) attending to the daily needs of the child, such as feeding, physical care, development, and grooming, supervision, spiritual growth and development, health care, day care, and engaging in other activities that are appropriate to the developmental level of the child and that are within the social and economic circumstances of the particular family;

(c) attending to adequate education for the child, including remedial or other education essential to the best interest of the child;

(d) ensuring the interactions and interrelationship of the child with the child's parents and siblings and with any other person who significantly affects the child's best interest; and

(e) exercising appropriate judgment regarding the child's welfare, consistent with the child's developmental level and the family's social and economic circumstances.

Based on the best interest of the child, a final parenting plan may include, at a minimum, provisions for:

(a) designation of a parent as custodian of the child, solely for the purposes of all other state and federal statutes that require a designation or determination of custody, but the designation may not affect either parent's rights and responsibilities under the parenting plan;

(b) designation of the legal residence of both parents and the child;

(c) a residential schedule specifying the periods of time during which the child will reside with each parent, including provisions for holidays, birthdays of family members, vacations, and other special occasions;

(d) finances to provide for the child's needs;

(e) any other factors affecting the physical and emotional health and well-being of the child;

(f) periodic review of the parenting plan when requested by either parent or the child or when circumstances arise that are foreseen by the parents as triggering a need for review, such as attainment by the child of a certain age or if a change in the child's residence is necessitated;

(g) sanctions that will apply if a parent fails to follow the terms of the parenting plan, including contempt of court;

(h) allocation of parental decision making authority regarding the child's education, spiritual development, and health care and physical growth;

(i) the method by which future disputes concerning the child will be resolved between the parents, other than court action; and

(j) the unique circumstances of the child or the family situation that the parents agree will facilitate a meaningful, ongoing relationship between the child and parents.

Each parent may make decisions regarding the day-to-day care and control of the child while the child is residing with that parent, and either parent may make emergency decisions affecting the child's safety or health. When mutual decision making is designated in the parenting plan but cannot be achieved regarding a particular issue, the parents shall make a good faith effort to resolve the issue through any dispute resolution process provided for in the final parenting plan.
                                        -From 40-4-234 of the Montana Code.

Nebraska
42-364 Action involving child support, child custody, parenting time, visitation, or other access; parenting plan; legal custody and physical custody determination;

rights of parents; child support; termination of parental rights; court; duties; modification proceedings; use of school records as evidence.

(1) In an action under Chapter 42 involving child support, child custody, parenting time, visitation, or other access, the parties and their counsel, if represented, shall develop a parenting plan as provided in the Parenting Act. If the parties and counsel do not develop a parenting plan, the complaint shall so indicate as provided in section 42-353 and before July 1, 2010, the case may be referred to mediation, specialized alternative dispute resolution, or other alternative dispute resolution process and on or after such date the case shall be referred to mediation or specialized alternative dispute resolution as provided in the Parenting Act. The decree in an action involving the custody of a minor child shall include the determination of legal custody and physical custody based upon the best interests of the child, as defined in the Parenting Act, and child support. Such determinations shall be made by incorporation into the decree of (a) a parenting plan developed by the parties, if approved by the court, or (b) a parenting plan developed by the court based upon evidence produced after a hearing in open court if no parenting plan is developed by the parties or the plan developed by the parties is not approved by the court. The decree shall conform to the Parenting Act. The social security number of each parent and the minor child shall be furnished to the clerk of the district court but shall not be disclosed or considered a public record.

(2) In determining legal custody or physical custody, the court shall not give preference to either parent based on the sex of the parent and, except as provided in section 43-2933, no presumption shall exist that either parent is more fit or suitable than the other. Custody shall be determined on the basis of the best interests of the child, as defined in the Parenting Act. Unless parental rights are terminated, both parents shall continue to have the rights stated in section 42-381.

(3) Custody of a minor child may be placed with both parents on a joint legal custody or joint physical custody basis, or both, (a) when both parents agree to such an arrangement in the parenting plan and the court determines that such an arrangement is in the best interests of the child or (b) if the court specifically finds, after a hearing in open court, that joint physical custody or joint legal custody, or both, is in the best interests of the minor child regardless of any parental agreement or consent.

(4) In determining the amount of child support to be paid by a parent, the court shall consider the earning capacity of each parent and the guidelines provided by the Supreme Court pursuant to section 42-364.16 for the establishment of child support obligations. Upon application, hearing, and presentation of evidence of an abusive disregard of the use of child support money paid by one party to the other, the court may require the party receiving such payment to file a verified report with the court, as often as the court requires, stating the manner in which such money is used. Child support paid to the party having custody of the minor child shall be the property of such party except as provided in section 43-512.07. The clerk of the district court shall maintain a record, separate from all other judgment dockets, of all decrees and orders in which the payment of child support or spousal support has been ordered, whether ordered by a district court,

county court, separate juvenile court, or county court sitting as a juvenile court. Orders for child support in cases in which a party has applied for services under Title IV-D of the federal Social Security Act, as amended, shall be reviewed as provided in sections 43-512.12 to 43-512.18.

(5) Whenever termination of parental rights is placed in issue:

(a) The court shall transfer jurisdiction to a juvenile court established pursuant to the Nebraska Juvenile Code unless a showing is made that the county court or district court is a more appropriate forum. In making such determination, the court may consider such factors as cost to the parties, undue delay, congestion of dockets, and relative resources available for investigative and supervisory assistance. A determination that the county court or district court is a more appropriate forum shall not be a final order for the purpose of enabling an appeal. If no such transfer is made, the court shall appoint an attorney as guardian ad litem to protect the interests of any minor child. The court may terminate the parental rights of one or both parents after notice and hearing when the court finds such action to be in the best interests of the minor child, as defined in the Parenting Act, and it appears by the evidence that one or more of the grounds for termination of parental rights stated in section 43-292 exist; and

(b) The court shall inform a parent who does not have legal counsel of the parent's right to retain counsel and of the parent's right to retain legal counsel at county expense if such parent is unable to afford legal counsel. If such parent is unable to afford legal counsel and requests the court to appoint legal counsel, the court shall immediately appoint an attorney to represent the parent in the termination proceedings. The court shall order the county to pay the attorney's fees and all reasonable expenses incurred by the attorney in protecting the rights of the parent. At such hearing, the guardian ad litem shall take all action necessary to protect the interests of the minor child. The court shall fix the fees and expenses of the guardian ad litem and tax the same as costs but may order the county to pay on finding the responsible party indigent and unable to pay.

(6) Modification proceedings relating to support, custody, parenting time, visitation, other access, or removal of children from the jurisdiction of the court shall be commenced by filing a complaint to modify. Modification of a parenting plan is governed by the Parenting Act. Proceedings to modify a parenting plan shall be commenced by filing a complaint to modify. Such actions may be referred to mediation, specialized alternative dispute resolution, or other alternative dispute resolution process before July 1, 2010, and on and after such date shall be referred to mediation or specialized alternative dispute resolution as provided in the Parenting Act. Service of process and other procedure shall comply with the requirements for a dissolution action.

(7) In any proceeding under this section relating to custody of a child of school age, certified copies of school records relating to attendance and academic progress of such child are admissible in evidence.

Nevada
How the Court Determines Child Custody.
In determining custody of a minor child in an action brought under this chapter, the sole consideration of the court is the best interest of the child. If it appears to the

court that joint custody would be in the best interest of the child, the court may grant custody to the parties jointly.

In determining the best interest of the child, the court shall consider, among other things:
(a) The wishes of the child if the child is of sufficient age and capacity to form an intelligent preference as to custody;
(b) Any nomination by a parent or a guardian for the child; and
(c) Whether either parent or any other person seeking custody has engaged in an act of domestic violence against the child, a parent of the child or any other person residing with the child.

A finding of domestic violence creates a rebuttable presumption that sole or joint custody of the child by the perpetrator of the domestic violence is not in the best interest of the child.

-From the Nevada Revised Statutes 125.480

Joint Custody.
There is a presumption that joint custody would be in the best interest of a minor child if the parents agree to an award of joint custody.

The court may award joint legal custody, without awarding joint physical custody, if the parents have agreed to joint legal custody.

-From the Nevada Revised Statutes 125.490

Removing the Child from the State.
If custody has been established, and the custodial parent intends to move outside of the state with the child, that parent must, as soon as possible and before the planned move, attempt to obtain the written consent of the noncustodial parent to move the child from this state. If the noncustodial parent refuses to give that consent, the custodial parent shall, before leaving this state with the child, petition the court for permission to move the child. The failure of a parent to comply with the provisions of this section may be considered as a factor if a change of custody is requested by the noncustodial parent.

-From the Nevada Revised Statutes 125C.200

New Hampshire
When determining a child custody award, New Hampshire laws consider the best interests of the child. There shall be a presumption, affecting the burden of proof, that joint legal custody is in the best interest of minor children if any of the following apply:
(a) Where the parents have agreed to an award of joint legal custody, or
(b) Upon the application of either parent for joint legal custody, in which case it may be awarded in the discretion of the court. To assist the court in making a determination whether an award of joint legal custody is appropriate, the court may appoint a guardian ad litem to represent the interests of the children.

(c) Where the court finds that abuse has occurred, the court shall consider such abuse as harmful to children in determining whether joint legal custody is appropriate. In such cases, the court shall make custody and visitation orders that best protect the children, or the abused spouse, or both.

"Joint legal custody" shall include all parental rights with the exception of physical custody which shall be awarded as the court deems most conducive to the benefit of the children.

-From 458:17 of the New Hampshire Statutes.

Allegations or evidence of specific acts of misconduct where child custody is an issue are only admissible when the misconduct is relevant to establish that parental custody would be detrimental to the child.

-From 458:7-a of the New Hampshire Statutes.

New Jersey
"Parent's Education program"
There is hereby established a mandatory education program to be known as the "Parents' Education Program." 2A:34-12.3.

Notice; Opportunity to be Heard; Joinder.
a. Before a child custody determination is made under this act, notice and an opportunity to be heard in accordance with the standards of section 8 of this act shall be given to all persons entitled to notice under the law of this State as in child custody proceedings between residents of this State, any parent whose parental rights have not been previously terminated, and any person having physical custody of the child.

b. This act does not govern the enforceability of a child custody determination made without notice and an opportunity to be heard.

c. The obligation to join a party and the right to intervene as a party in a child custody proceeding under this act are governed by the law of this State as in child custody proceedings between residents of this State.

L.2004,c.147,s.17.

New Mexico
Child Custody Guidelines.
In determining custody of a minor child, New Mexico laws require the court, if the minor is under the age of fourteen, to determine custody in accordance with the best interests of the child. The court shall consider all relevant factors including, but not limited to:
(1) the wishes of the child's parent or parents as to his custody;
(2) the wishes of the child as to his custodian;
(3) the interaction and interrelationship of the child with his parents, his siblings and any other person who may significantly affect the child's best interest;
(4) the child's adjustment to his home, school and community; and

(5) the mental and physical health of all individuals involved.

If the minor is fourteen years of age or older, the court shall consider the desires of the minor as to with whom he wishes to live before awarding custody of such minor. The court shall not prefer one parent as a custodian solely because of gender.

Joint Custody.
When the parents agree to a form of custody, the court should award custody consistent with the agreement unless the court determines that such agreement is not in the best interests of the child. There shall be a presumption that joint custody is in the best interests of a child in an initial custody determination. In determining whether a joint custody order is in the best interests of the child, in addition to the factors listed above, the court shall consider the following factors:
(1) whether the child has established a close relationship with each parent;
(2) whether each parent is capable of providing adequate care for the child through-out each period of responsibility, including arranging for the child's care by others as needed;
(3) whether each parent is willing to accept all responsibilities of parenting, includ-ing a willingness to accept care of the child at specified times and to relinquish care to the other parent at specified times;
(4) whether the child can best maintain and strengthen a relationship with both parents through predictable, frequent contact and whether the child's develop-ment will profit from such involvement and influence from both parents;
(5) whether each parent is able to allow the other to provide care without intrusion, that is, to respect the other's parental rights and responsibilities and right to pri-vacy;
(6) the suitability of a parenting plan for the implementation of joint custody, preferably, although not necessarily, one arrived at through parental agreement;
(7) geographic distance between the parents' residences;
(8) willingness or ability of the parents to communicate, cooperate or agree on issues regarding the child's needs; and
(9) whether a judicial adjudication has been made in a prior or the present proceed-ing that either parent or other person seeking custody has engaged in one or more acts of domestic abuse against the child, a parent of the child or other household member. If a determination is made that domestic abuse has occurred, the court shall set forth findings that the custody or visitation ordered by the court adequately protects the child, the abused parent or other household mem-ber.

Joint Custody - Definitions.
An award of joint custody means that:
(1) each parent shall have significant, well-defined periods of responsibility for the child;
(2) each parent shall have, and be allowed and expected to carry out, responsibility for the child's financial, physical, emotional and developmental needs during that parent's periods of responsibility;

(3) the parents shall consult with each other on major decisions involving the child before implementing those decisions; that is, neither parent shall make a decision or take an action which results in a major change in a child's life until the matter has been discussed with the other parent and the parents agree. If the parents, after discussion, cannot agree and if one parent wishes to effect a major change while the other does not wish the major change to occur, then no change shall occur until the issue has been resolved as provided in this subsection;

(4) the following guidelines apply to major changes in a child's life:

    (a) if either parent plans to change his home city or state of residence, he shall provide to the other parent thirty days' notice in writing stating the date and destination of move;

    (b) the religious denomination and religious activities, or lack thereof, which were being practiced during the marriage should not be changed unless the parties agree or it has been otherwise resolved as provided in this subsection;

    (c) both parents shall have access to school records, teachers and activities. The type of education, public or private, which was in place during the marriage should continue, whenever possible, and school districts should not be changed unless the parties agree or it has been otherwise resolved as provided in this subsection;

    (d) both parents shall have access to medical and dental treatment providers and records. Each parent has authority to make emergency medical decisions. Neither parent may contract for major elective medical or dental treatment unless both parents agree or it has been otherwise resolved as provided in this subsection; and

    (e) both parents may attend the child's public activities and both parents should know the necessary schedules. Whatever recreational activities the child participated in during the marriage should continue with the child's agreement, regardless of which of the parents has physical custody. Also, neither parent may enroll the child in a new recreational activity unless the parties agree or it has been otherwise resolved as provided in this subsection; and

(5) decisions regarding major changes in a child's life may be decided by:

    (a) agreement between the joint custodial parents;

    (b) requiring that the parents seek family counseling, conciliation or mediation service to assist in resolving their differences;

    (c) agreement by the parents to submit the dispute to binding arbitration;

    (d) allocating ultimate responsibility for a particular major decision area to one legal custodian;

    (e) terminating joint custody and awarding sole custody to one person;

    (f) reference to a master pursuant to Rule 53 [Rule 1-053 NMRA] of the Rules of Civil Procedure for the District Courts; or

    (g) the district court.

-From 40-4-9 of the New Mexico Statutes.

Access to Records.
Notwithstanding any other provisions of law, access to records and information pertaining to a minor child, including medical, dental and school records, shall not be

denied to a parent because that parent is not the child's physical custodial parent or because that parent is not a joint custodial parent.

New York

New York laws will take into consideration the best interests of the child when determining custody, but there are no specific guidelines in the statutes to determine custody. It will be decided on a case-by-case basis.

North Carolina

An order for custody of a minor child shall award the custody of such child to whom will best promote the interest and welfare of the child. In making the determination, the court shall consider all relevant factors including acts of domestic violence between the parties, the safety of the child, and the safety of either party from domestic violence by the other party and shall make findings accordingly. An order for custody must include findings of fact which support the determination of what is in the best interest of the child. Between the mother and father, whether natural or adoptive, no presumption shall apply as to who will better promote the interest and welfare of the child. Joint custody to the parents shall be considered upon the request of either parent.

Absent an order of the court to the contrary, each parent shall have equal access to the records of the minor child involving the health, education, and welfare of the child.

-From Section §50-13.2 of the North Carolina Statutes.

North Dakota

North Dakota laws require the court to consider the best interests and welfare of the minor child when awarding child custody. There is no presumption on the basis of gender between the mother and father, whether natural or adoptive, which parent will better promote the best interests and welfare of the child.
The best interests and welfare of the child is determined by the court's consideration and evaluation of all factors including:
a. The love, affection, and other emotional ties existing between the parents and child.
b. The capacity and disposition of the parents to give the child love, affection, and guidance and to continue the education of the child.
c. The disposition of the parents to provide the child with food, clothing, medical care, or other remedial care recognized and permitted under the laws of this state in lieu of medical care, and other material needs.
d. The length of time the child has lived in a stable satisfactory environment and the desirability of maintaining continuity.
e. The permanence, as a family unit, of the existing or proposed custodial home.
f. The moral fitness of the parents.
g. The mental and physical health of the parents.
h. The home, school, and community record of the child.
i. The reasonable preference of the child, if the court deems the child to be of sufficient intelligence, understanding, and experience to express a preference.

j. Evidence of domestic violence. If the court finds credible evidence that domestic violence has occurred, and there exists one incident of domestic violence which resulted in serious bodily injury or involved the use of a dangerous weapon, or there exists a pattern of domestic violence within a reasonable time proximate to the proceeding, this creates a rebuttable presumption that a parent who has perpetrated domestic violence may not be awarded sole or joint custody of a child. This presumption may be overcome only by clear and convincing evidence that the best interests of the child require that parent's participation as a custodial parent. The fact that the abused parent suffers from the effects of the abuse may not be grounds for denying that parent custody.

k. The interaction and relationship, or the potential for interaction, of the child with any person who resides in, is present, or frequents the household of a parent and who may significantly affect the child's best interests. The court shall consider that person's history of inflicting, or tendency to inflict, physical harm, bodily injury, assault, or the fear of physical harm, bodily injury, or assault, on other persons.

l. The making of false allegations not made in good faith, by one parent against the other, of harm to a child.

m. Any other factors considered by the court to be relevant to a particular child custody dispute.

-From 14-09-06.1 & 14-09-06.2 of the North Carolina Statutes

Parental Rights and Duties.
Each parent of a child has the following custody and visitation rights and duties, unless otherwise ordered by the court:

a. Right to access and obtain copies of the child's educational, medical, dental, religious, insurance, and other records or information.

b. Right to attend educational conferences concerning the child. This right does not require any school to hold a separate conference with each parent.

c. Right to reasonable access to the child by written, telephonic, and electronic means.

d. Duty to inform the other parent as soon as reasonably possible of a serious accident or serious illness for which the child receives health care treatment. The parent shall provide to the other parent a description of the serious accident or serious illness, the time of the serious accident or serious illness, and the name and location of the treating health care provider.

e. Duty to immediately inform the other parent of a change in residential telephone number and address.

f. Duty to keep the other parent informed of the name and address of the school the child attends.

-From 14-09-28 of the North Dakota Statutes.

Ohio
Preference of the Child.
When making the allocation of the parental rights and responsibilities for the care of the children under this section, the court shall take into account that which would be in the best interest of the children. In determining the child's best interest for

purposes of making its allocation of the parental rights and responsibilities for the care of the child and for purposes of resolving any issues related to the making of that allocation, the court, in its discretion, may and, upon the request of either party, shall interview in chambers any or all of the involved children regarding their wishes and concerns with respect to the allocation.

No person shall obtain or attempt to obtain from a child a written or recorded statement or affidavit setting forth the child's wishes and concerns regarding the allocation of parental rights and responsibilities concerning the child. No court, in determining the child's best interest for purposes of making its allocation of the parental rights and responsibilities for the care of the child or for purposes of resolving any issues related to the making of that allocation, shall accept or consider a written or recorded statement or affidavit that purports to set forth the child's wishes and concerns regarding those matters.

-From Section §3109.04 of the Ohio Statutes.

Joint Custody Plan.
If both parents jointly request the court to grant both parents shared parental rights and responsibilities, the court shall review the parents' plan to determine if it is in the best interest of the children. If the court determines that the plan is in the best interest of the children, the court shall approve it. If the court determines that the plan or any part of the plan is not in the best interest of the children, the court shall require the parents to make appropriate changes to the plan to meet the court's objections to it.

If each parent requests the court to grant both parents shared parental rights and responsibilities and each also files a separate plan, the court shall review each plan filed to determine if either is in the best interest of the children. If the court determines that one of the filed plans is in the best interest of the children, the court may approve the plan. If the court determines that neither filed plan is in the best interest of the children, the court may order each parent to submit appropriate changes to the parent's plan or both of the filed plans to meet the court's objections, or may select one of the filed plans and order each parent to submit appropriate changes to the selected plan to meet the court's objections.

If each parent requests the court to grant both parents shared parental rights and responsibilities but only one parent files a plan, or if only one parent request the court to grant both parents shared parental rights and responsibilities, the court in the best interest of the children may order the other parent to file a plan for shared parenting.

Whenever possible, the court shall require that a shared parenting plan ensure the opportunity for both parents to have frequent and continuing contact with the child, unless frequent and continuing contact with any parent would not be in the best interest of the child. -From Section §3109.04 of the Ohio Statutes.

Best Interest of the Child.
In determining the best interest of a child, the court shall consider all relevant factors, including, but not limited to:
(a) The wishes of the child's parents regarding the child's care;
(b) If the court has interviewed the child in chambers pursuant to division (B) of this section regarding the child's wishes and concerns as to the allocation of parental rights and responsibilities concerning the child, the wishes and concerns of the child, as expressed to the court;
(c) The child's interaction and interrelationship with the child's parents, siblings, and any other person who may significantly affect the child's best interest;
(d) The child's adjustment to the child's home, school, and community;
(e) The mental and physical health of all persons involved in the situation;
(f) The parent more likely to honor and facilitate court-approved parenting time rights or visitation and companionship rights;
(g) Whether either parent has failed to make all child support payments, including all arrearages, that are required of that parent pursuant to a child support order under which that parent is an obligor;
(h) Whether there is reason to believe that either parent has acted in a manner resulting in a child being an abused child or a neglected child;
(i) Whether the residential parent or one of the parents subject to a shared parenting decree has continuously and willfully denied the other parent's right to parenting time in accordance with an order of the court;
(j) Whether either parent has established a residence, or is planning to establish a residence, outside this state.

In determining whether shared parenting is in the best interest of the children, the court shall consider all relevant factors, including, but not limited to, the factors above, the factors enumerated in section 3119.23 of the Revised Code, and all of the following factors:
(a) The ability of the parents to cooperate and make decisions jointly, with respect to the children;
(b) The ability of each parent to encourage the sharing of love, affection, and contact between the child and the other parent;
(c) Any history of, or potential for, child abuse, spouse abuse, other domestic violence, or parental kidnapping by either parent;
(d) The geographic proximity of the parents to each other, as the proximity relates to the practical considerations of shared parenting;
(e) The recommendation of the guardian ad litem of the child, if the child has a guardian ad litem.
When allocating parental rights and responsibilities for the care of children, the court shall not give preference to a parent because of that parent's financial status or condition.

-From Section §3109.04 of the Ohio Statutes.

Oklahoma
Best Interest of Child.
It is the policy of the state of Oklahoma to assure that minor children have frequent

and continuing contact with parents who have shown the ability to act in the best interests of their children and to encourage parents to share in the rights and responsibilities of rearing their children after the parents have separated or dissolved their marriage. In awarding the custody of a minor child, the court shall consider what appears to be in the best interests of the physical and mental and moral welfare of the child. There shall be neither a legal preference nor a presumption for or against joint legal custody, joint physical custody, or sole custody.

When awarding custody to either parent, the court shall consider, among other facts, which parent is more likely to allow the child or children frequent and continuing contact with the noncustodial parent, and shall not prefer a parent as a custodian of the child because of the gender of that parent. Except for good cause shown, a pattern of failure to allow court-ordered visitation may be determined to be contrary to the best interests of the child. -From Sections §43-109 through 43-112.

Preference of Child.
In any action or proceeding in which a court must determine custody or limits of or period of visitation, the child may express a preference as to which of its parents the child wishes to have custody. The court shall determine whether the best interest of the child will be served by the child's expression of preference as to which parent should have custody or limits of or period of visitation rights of either parent. If the court so finds, the child may express such preference or give other testimony.

If the child is of a sufficient age to form an intelligent preference, the court shall consider the expression of preference or other testimony of the child in determining custody or limits of or period of visitation.

The court shall not be bound by the child's choice and may take other facts into consideration in awarding custody or limits of or period of visitation. However, if the child is of a sufficient age to form an intelligent preference and the court does not follow the expression of preference of the child as to custody, or limits of visitation, the court shall make specific findings of fact supporting such action if requested by either party. There shall be a rebuttable presumption that a child who is 12 years of age or older is of a sufficient age to form an intelligent preference.
-From Section §43 113 of the Oklahoma Statutes.

Denial of Visitation, Nonpayment of Child Support.
Except for good cause shown, when a noncustodial parent who is ordered to pay child support and who is awarded visitation rights fails to pay child support, the custodial parent shall not refuse to honor the noncustodial parent's visitation rights. When a custodial parent refuses to honor a noncustodial parent's visitation rights, the noncustodial parent shall not fail to pay any ordered child support or alimony.
-From Section §43-111.1 of the Oklahoma Statutes.

Relocation.
"Relocation" means a change in the principal residence of a child over 75 miles from

the child's principal residence for a period of 60 days or more, but does not include a temporary absence from the principal residence.

Except as otherwise provided by this section, a person who has the right to establish the principal residence of the child shall notify every other person entitled to visitation with the child of a proposed relocation of the child's principal residence as required by this section, and an adult entitled to visitation with a child shall notify every other person entitled to custody of or visitation with the child of an intended change in the primary residence address of the adult as required by this section.

A person required to give notice of a proposed relocation or change of residence address under this subsection has a continuing duty to provide a change in or addition to the information required by this subsection as that information becomes known.

The court may consider a failure to provide notice of a proposed relocation of a child as provided by this section as:
a. a factor in making its determination regarding the relocation of a child,
b. a factor in determining whether custody or visitation should be modified,
c. a basis for ordering the return of the child if the relocation has taken place without notice, and
d. sufficient cause to order the person seeking to relocate the child to pay reasonable expenses and attorney fees incurred by the person objecting to the relocation.

In reaching its decision regarding a proposed relocation, the court shall consider the following factors:
a. the nature, quality, extent of involvement, and duration of the child's relationship with the person proposing to relocate and with the nonrelocating person, siblings, and other significant persons in the child's life,
b. the age, developmental stage, needs of the child, and the likely impact the relocation will have on the child's physical, educational, and emotional development, taking into consideration any special needs of the child,
c. the feasibility of preserving the relationship between the nonrelocating person and the child through suitable visitation arrangements, considering the logistics and financial circumstances of the parties,
d. the child's preference, taking into consideration the age and maturity of the child,
e. whether there is an established pattern of conduct of the person seeking the relocation, either to promote or thwart the relationship of the child and the nonrelocating person,
f. whether the relocation of the child will enhance the general quality of life for both the custodial party seeking the relocation and the child, including but not limited to financial or emotional benefit or educational opportunity,
g. the reasons of each person for seeking or opposing the relocation, and
h. any other factor affecting the best interest of the child.

-From Section §43-112.3 of the Oklahoma Statutes.

Oregon
Child Custody Guidelines.
Oregon laws require the court to give primary consideration to the best interests and welfare of the child when making a child custody determination. In determining the best interests and welfare of the child, the court shall consider the following relevant factors:

(a) The emotional ties between the child and other family members;
(b) The interest of the parties in and attitude toward the child;
(c) The desirability of continuing an existing relationship;
(d) The abuse of one parent by the other;
(e) The preference for the primary caregiver of the child, if the caregiver is deemed fit by the court; and
(f) The willingness and ability of each parent to facilitate and encourage a close and continuing relationship between the other parent and the child, unless there has been sexual assault or a pattern of abuse against the parent or the child that will endanger the health or safety of either parent or the child.

The best interests and welfare of the child shall not be determined by isolating any one of these factors, and relying on it to the exclusion of other factors. However, if a parent has committed abuse, there is a rebuttable presumption that it is not in the best interests and welfare of the child to award sole or joint custody of the child to the parent who committed the abuse.

The court shall consider the conduct, marital status, income, social environment or life style of either party only if it is shown that any of these factors are causing or may cause emotional or physical damage to the child.

No preference in custody shall be given to either parent on the basis of that parent's sex.

Oregon laws do not allow the court to hear evidence of specific acts of misconduct, unless the misconduct is relevant to determining child custody.
                              -From 107.036 & 107.137 of the Oregon Statutes.

Parenting Plans.
The parties should file a parenting plan to be included in the judgment. A parenting plan may be either general or detailed.

A general parenting plan must set forth the minimum amount of parenting time and access a noncustodial parent is entitled to have, and how parental responsibilities will be shared. The parents may develop a more detailed agreement on an informal basis.

If the parents wish to file a more detailed parenting plan with the court, this plan may include, but need not be limited to, provisions relating to:
(a) Residential schedule;
(b) Holiday, birthday and vacation planning;

(c) Weekends, including holidays, and school in-service days preceding or following weekends;
(d) Decision-making and responsibility;
(e) Information sharing and access;
(f) Relocation of parents;
(g) Telephone access;
(h) Transportation; and
(i) Methods for resolving disputes.

-From 107.102 of the Oregon Statutes.

Parental Rights.
Unless otherwise ordered by the court, when one parent has sole custody, the other parent will still have the following rights, to the same extent as the custodial parent has the following rights:
(1) To inspect and receive school records and to consult with school staff concerning the child's welfare and education;
(2) To inspect and receive governmental agency and law enforcement records concerning the child;
(3) To consult with any person who may provide care or treatment for the child and to inspect and receive the child's medical, dental and psychological records;
(4) To authorize emergency medical, dental, psychological, psychiatric or other health care for the child if the custodial parent is, for practical purposes, un-available; or
(5) To apply to be the child's conservator, guardian ad litem or both.

-From 107.154 of the Oregon Statutes.

Moving with the Child & Notice of Changes.
Neither parent may move to a residence more than 60 miles from the other parent without giving the other parent reasonable notice of the move, and providing a copy of such notice to the court.

Unless otherwise ordered by the court, both parents shall have a continuing responsibility to provide addresses and contact telephone numbers to the other parent and to immediately notify the other parent of any emergency circumstances or substantial changes in the health of the child.

-From 107.159 & 107.164 of the Oregon Statutes.

Pennsylvania
Child custody issues, involve the court making a choice about the parent who will encourage, permit and actually allow the frequent and also the continued relation-ship, including physical access, between the child and the noncustodial parent. Sole custody is awarded if the court determines that it is in the child's best interest. Shared custody is possible when it in the best interest of the child. The process of shared custody involves an application and agreement by both parents.

Title 23 - Section: 5303

Rhode Island

In regulating the custody of the children, the court shall provide for the reasonable right of visitation by the natural parent not having custody of the children, except upon the showing of cause why the right should not be granted. The court shall mandate compliance with its order by both the custodial parent and the children. In the event of noncompliance, the noncustodial parent may file a motion for contempt in family court. Upon a finding by the court that its order for visitation has not been complied with, the court shall exercise its discretion in providing a remedy, and define the noncustodial parent's visitation in detail. However, if a second finding of noncompliance by the court is made, the court shall consider this to be grounds for a change of custody to the noncustodial parent.

In regulating the custody and determining the best interests of children, the fact that a parent is receiving public assistance shall not be a factor in awarding custody.

§ 15-5-24.1 Visitation rights of grandparents. – The court may, upon miscellaneous petition of a grandparent whose child is deceased, grant reasonable visitation rights of the grandchild or grandchildren to the grandparent, whether or not any divorce or custody proceedings were ever commenced, and may issue all necessary orders to enforce visitation rights.

South Carolina
SECTION 63-15-30. Child's preference.
In determining the best interests of the child, the court must consider the child's reasonable preference for custody. The court shall place weight upon the preference based upon the child's age, experience, maturity, judgment, and ability to express a preference.

SECTION 63-15-40. Consideration of domestic violence.
(A) In making a decision regarding custody of a minor child, in addition to other existing factors specified by law, the court must give weight to evidence of domestic violence as defined in Section 16-25-20 or Section 16-25-65 including, but not limited to:
   (1) physical or sexual abuse; and
   (2) if appropriate, evidence of which party was the primary aggressor, as defined in Section 16-25-70.
(B) The absence or relocation from the home by a person, against whom an act of domestic violence has been perpetrated, if that person is not the primary aggressor, must not be considered by the court to be sufficient cause, absent other factors, to deny custody of the minor child to that person.

SECTION 63-15-60. De facto custodian.
(A) For purposes of this section, "de facto custodian" means, unless the context requires otherwise, a person who has been shown by clear and convincing evidence to have been the primary caregiver

for and financial supporter of a child who:
   (1) has resided with the person for a period of six months or more
       if the child is under three years of age; or
   (2) has resided with the person for a period of one year or more if
       the child is three years of age or older.

   Any period of time after a legal proceeding has been commenced by a parent
   seeking to regain custody of the child must not be included in determining
   whether the child has resided with the person for the required minimum period.

(B) A person is not a de facto custodian of a child until the court
    determines by clear and convincing evidence that the person
    meets the definition of de facto custodian with respect to that
    child. If the court determines a person is a de facto custodian
    of a child, that person has standing to seek visitation or
    custody of that child.

(C) The family court may grant visitation or custody of a child to
    the de facto custodian if it finds by clear and convincing evidence
    that the child's natural parents are unfit or that other compelling
    circumstances exist.

(D) No proceeding to establish whether a person is a de facto custom
    dian may be brought concerning a child in the custody of the
    Department of Social Services.

(E) If the court has determined by clear and convincing evidence that a
    person is a de facto custodian, the court must join that person in the
    action as a party needed for just adjudication under the South
    Carolina Rules of Civil Procedure.

South Dakota

25-5-7. **Parents equally entitled to custody** and earnings of child born in
wedlock. Subject to the court's right to award custody of the child to either parent,
considering the best interest of the child as to its temporal, mental, and moral welfare
the father and mother of any minor child born in wedlock are equally entitled to the
child's custody, service, and earnings.

25-5-7.1. Order for joint legal custody--Factors for court's consideration. In any
custody dispute between parents, the court may order joint legal custody so that both
parents retain full parental rights and responsibilities with respect to their child and
so that both parents must confer on major decisions affecting the welfare of the child.
In ordering joint legal custody, the court may consider the expressed desires of the
parents and may grant to one party the ultimate responsibility over specific aspects of
the child's welfare or may divide those aspects between the parties based on the best
interest of the child. If it appears to the court to be in the best interest of the child, the
court may order, or the parties may agree, how any such responsibility shall be
divided. Such areas of responsibility may include primary physical residence,
education, medical and dental care, and any other responsibilities which the court
finds unique to a particular family or in the best interest of the child.

25-5-7.2.　Residential parent to make routine decisions concerning child. During the time a child, over whom the court has ordered joint legal custody to both parents, resides with either parent, that parent shall decide all routine matters concerning the child.

25-5-7.3.　Parents to have equal access to records pertaining to child--Name and address of both parents to be listed. Access to records and information pertaining to a minor child, including, but not limited to, medical, dental, orthodontia, optometric and similar health care, and school records shall be made equally available to both parents. Counseling, psychiatric, psychotherapy, and other records subject to confidentiality or privilege shall only be released in accordance with state and federal law; but, if available to one parent, shall be available to both. The parents shall make reasonable efforts to ensure that the name and address of the other parent is listed on all such records.

25-5-10.1.　Best interest of child not presumed--Change of custody. Notwithstanding any initial entitlement to custody pursuant to § 25-5-10, there is no legal presumption that such custody is in the best interest of the child, nor is a change of circumstances required for a change of the initial custody as determined by § 25-5-10.

25-5-13.　Power to change residence of child--Restraining power of circuit court. A parent entitled to the custody of a child has the right to change his residence, subject to the power of the circuit court to restrain a removal which would prejudice the rights or welfare of the child.

25-4A-11.　Plaintiff in custody action to file and serve guidelines--Guidelines as court order-- Custody of minors. Upon the filing of a summons and complaint for divorce or separate maintenance or any other custody action or proceeding, the plaintiff shall also file and serve upon the defendant a copy of the standard guidelines. The standard guidelines attached to the summons shall become an order of the court upon fulfillment of the requirements of service. Any minor child of the marriage shall remain in the custody of the parent who has been the primary caregiver for the minor child for the majority of time in the twelve months preceding the filing of the summons and complaint, unless the parties agree otherwise. The standard guidelines shall apply and continue in effect, unless the parties agree, or the court orders otherwise. Imposition of the standard guidelines creates no presumption as to who may be awarded custody at any hearing. SL 2002, ch 125, § 3; SL 2008, ch 127, § 1.

Tennessee
Jurisdiction.
In order for a court to decide custody of your children, whether by agreement of the spouses or by decision of the court, that court must have jurisdiction. Except as otherwise provided in §36-6-219 regarding Temporary Emergency Jurisdiction, a court of the state of Tennessee has jurisdiction to make an initial child custody determination only if:

(1) The state of Tennessee is the home state of the child on the date of the commencement of the proceeding, or was the home state of the child within six months before the commencement of the proceeding and the child is absent from Tennessee but a parent or person acting as a parent continues to live in Tennessee. "Home state" means the state in which a child lived with a parent or a person acting as a parent for at least six consecutive months immediately before the commencement of a child custody proceeding, or in the case of a child less than six months of age, the state in which the child lived from birth. A period of temporary absence of any of the mentioned persons is part of the period;

(2) A court of another state does not have jurisdiction, or a court of the home state of the child has declined to exercise jurisdiction on the ground that the state of Tennessee is the more appropriate forum, and:

(A) The child and the child's parents, or the child and at least one parent or a person acting as a parent, have a significant connection with this state other than mere physical presence; and

(B) Substantial evidence is available in this state concerning the child's care, protection, training, and personal relationships;

(3) All courts having jurisdiction have declined to exercise jurisdiction on the ground that a court of this state is the more appropriate forum to determine the custody of the child under §36-6-221 or §36-6-222; or

(4) No court of any other state would have jurisdiction.

-From Sections §36-6-205 and §36-6-216 of the Tennessee Code.

Best Interests of the Child.

In a suit for annulment, divorce, separate maintenance, or in any other proceeding requiring the court to make a custody determination regarding a minor child, such determination shall be made upon the basis of the best interest of the child. The court shall consider all relevant factors including the following where applicable:

(1) The love, affection and emotional ties existing between the parents and child;

(2) The disposition of the parents to provide the child with food, clothing, medical care, education and other necessary care and the degree to which a parent has been the primary caregiver;

(3) The importance of continuity in the child's life and the length of time the child has lived in a stable, satisfactory environment; provided, that where there is a finding, under § 36-6-106(a)(8), of child abuse, as defined in §§ 39-15-401 or 39-15-402, or child sexual abuse, as defined in § 37-1-602, by one (1) parent, and that a non-perpetrating parent has relocated in order to flee the perpetrating parent, that such relocation shall not weigh against an award of custody;

(4) The stability of the family unit of the parents;

(5) The mental and physical health of the parents;

(6) The home, school and community record of the child;

(7) The reasonable preference of the child if 12 years of age or older. The court may hear the preference of a younger child upon request. The preferences of older children should normally be given greater weight than those of younger children;

(8) Evidence of physical or emotional abuse to the child, to the other parent or to any other person;

(9) The character and behavior of any other person who resides in or frequents the home of a parent and such person's interactions with the child; and

(10) Each parent's past and potential for future performance of parenting responsibilities, including the willingness and ability of each of the parents to facilitate and encourage a close and continuing parent-child relationship between the child and the other parent, consistent with the best interest of the child.

It is the legislative intent that the gender of the party seeking custody shall not give rise to a presumption of parental fitness or cause a presumption or constitute a factor in favor or against the award of custody to such party.

The court shall approve agreements of the parties allocating parenting responsibilities, or specifying rules, if it finds that the agreement is consistent with any limitations on a parent's decision-making authority mandated by §36-6-406; the agreement is knowing and voluntary; and the agreement is in the best interest of the child.

-From Section §36-6-101, §36-6-106, and §36-6-407 of the Tennessee Code.

Designation of Custodian.

Solely for the purpose of all other state and federal statutes and any applicable policies of insurance that require a designation or determination of custody, a parenting plan shall designate the parent with whom the child is scheduled to reside a majority of the time as the custodian of the child; provided, that this designation shall not affect either parent's rights and responsibilities under the parenting plan. In the absence of such a designation, the parent with whom the child is scheduled to reside a majority of the time shall be deemed to be the custodian for the purposes of such federal and state statutes.

-From Section §36-6-410 of the Tennessee Code.

Rights of Each Parent.

Except when the court finds it not to be in the best interests of the child, each parent has the following rights during periods when the child is not in that parent's possession:

(A) The right to unimpeded telephone conversations with the child at least twice a week at reasonable times and for reasonable durations;

(B) The right to send mail to the child that the other parent shall not open or censor;

(C) The right to receive notice and relevant information as soon as practicable but within twenty-four (24) hours of any event of hospitalization, major illness or death of the child;

(D) The right to receive directly from the child's school records, names of teachers, class schedules, standardized test scores, and any other records customarily made available to parents, upon written request that includes a current mailing address and upon payment of reasonable costs of duplicating;

(E) Unless otherwise provided by law, the right to receive copies of the child's medical, health or other treatment records directly from the physician or health care provider who provided such treatment or health care upon written request that contains a current mailing address and upon payment of reasonable costs of duplication; provided, that no person who receives the mailing address of a parent as a result of this requirement shall provide such address to the other parent or a third person;

(F) The right to be free of unwarranted derogatory remarks made about such parent or such parent's family by the other parent to or in the presence of the child;

(G) The right to be given at least forty-eight (48) hours notice, whenever possible, of all extra-curricular activities, and the opportunity to participate or observe, including, but not limited to, the following:

(i) School activities;

(ii) Athletic activities;

(iii) Church activities; and

(iv) Other activities as to which parental participation or observation would be appropriate;

(H) The right to receive from the other parent, in the event the other parent leaves the state with the minor child or children for more than two (2) days, an itinerary including telephone numbers for use in the event of an emergency; and

(I) The right of access and participation in education, including the right of access to the minor child or children for lunch and other activities, on the same basis that is provided to all parents, provided the participation or access is reasonable and does not interfere with day-to-day operations or with the child's educational performance.

-From Section §36-6-101 of the Tennessee Code.

Visitation.

After making an award of custody, the court shall, upon request of the non-custodial parent, grant such rights of visitation as will enable the child and the non-custodial parent to maintain a parent-child relationship unless the court finds, after a hearing, that visitation is likely to endanger the child's physical or emotional health.

In granting any such rights of visitation, the court shall designate in which parent's home each minor child shall reside on given days of the year, including provisions for holidays, birthdays of family members, vacations and other special occasions.

-From Section §36-6-301 of the Tennessee Code.

Access to Records.

A copy of a child's medical and school records shall be furnished to the non-custodial parent upon written request, unless furnished with a court order closing the records.

-From Sections §36-6-103 and §36-6-104 of the Tennessee Code.

Relocation.

If a parent who is spending intervals of time with a child desires to relocate outside the state or more than 100 miles from the other parent within the state, the relocating parent shall send a notice to the other parent at the other parent's last known address by registered or certified mail. Unless excused by the court for exigent circumstances, the notice shall be mailed not later than 60 days prior to the move.

The court shall determine whether or not to permit relocation of the child based upon the best interests of the child. The court shall consider all relevant factors including the factors listed in §36-6-108 of the Tennessee Code.

-From Section §36-6-108 of the Tennessee Code.

Texas
Physical Custody.

Texas uses the term "possessory conservator" to describe which parent will have physical custody of a minor child or children. Texas uses a "standard possession order" as a guideline to determine visitation with the minor child(ren). The terms of the standard possession order can be found in Section 153.312-153.316 of the Texas Family Code.

The guidelines established in the standard possession order are intended to guide the courts in ordering the terms and conditions for possession of a child by a parent named as a possessory conservator or as the minimum possession for a joint managing conservator. There is a rebuttable presumption that the standard possession order provides reasonable minimum possession of a child for a parent named as a possessory conservator or joint managing conservator; and is in the best interest of the child. However, the court may render an order for periods of possession of a child that vary from the standard possession order based on the agreement of the parties.

To promote the amicable settlement of disputes between the parties to a suit, the parties may enter into a written agreed parenting plan containing provisions for conservatorship and possession of the child and for modification of the parenting plan, including variations from the standard possession order. If the court finds that the agreed parenting plan is in the child's best interest, the court shall render an order in accordance with the parenting plan. If the court finds the agreed parenting plan is not in the child's best interest, the court may request the parties to submit a revised parenting plan or the court may render an order for the conservatorship and possession of the child.

The public policy of the state of Texas is to:
(1) assure that children will have frequent and continuing contact with parents who have shown the ability to act in the best interest of the child;
(2) provide a safe, stable, and nonviolent environment for the child; and
(3) encourage parents to share in the rights and duties of raising their child after the parents have separated or dissolved their marriage.

The best interest of the child shall always be the primary consideration of the court in determining the issues of conservatorship and possession of and access to the child.

The court shall consider the qualifications of the parties without regard to their marital status or to the sex of the party or the child in determining:

(1) which party to appoint as sole managing conservator;
(2) whether to appoint a party as joint managing conservator; and
(3) the terms and conditions of conservatorship and possession of and
     access to the child.
 -From Sections 153.001 through 153.007 and 153.251 through 153.255 of the Texas
Family Code.

Legal Custody.
Texas uses the term "managing conservator" to describe which parent will have legal
custody of the minor child(ren). The court may appoint a sole managing conservator
or may appoint joint managing conservators. In determining whether to appoint a
party as a sole or joint managing conservator, the court shall consider evidence of
abuse. It is a rebuttable presumption that the appointment of the parents of a child as
joint managing conservators is in the best interest of the child. A finding of a history
of family violence involving the parents of a child removes the presumption under
this subsection.

The parents may file a written parenting plan with the court if they agree to be joint
managing conservators or if they agree which parent will be sole managing conservator. If a written agreed parenting plan is not filed with the court, the court may
render an order appointing the parents joint managing conservators only if the
appointment is in the best interest of the child, considering the following factors:
(1) whether the physical, psychological, or emotional needs and development of the
     child will benefit from the appointment of joint managing conservators;
(2) the ability of the parents to give first priority to the welfare of the child and reach
     shared decisions in the child's best interest;
(3) whether each parent can encourage and accept a positive relationship between the
     child and the other parent;
(4) whether both parents participated in child rearing before the filing of the suit;
(5) the geographical proximity of the parents' residences;
(6) if the child is 12 years of age or older, the child's preference, if any, regarding the
     person to have the exclusive right to designate the primary residence of the
     child; and
(7) any other relevant factor.
 -From Section 153.004, 153.005, 153.131, and 153.154 of the Texas Family Code.

Preference of the Child.
A child 12 years of age or older may file with the court in writing the name of the
person who is the child's preference to have the exclusive right to designate the
primary residence of the child, subject to the approval of the court.
                              -From Section 153.008 of the Texas Family Code.

Rights of Parent Appointed Conservator.
Unless limited by court order, a parent appointed as a sole or co-conservator of a
child has at all times the right:
(1) to receive information from any other conservator of the child concerning the
     health, education, and welfare of the child;

(2) to confer with the other parent to the extent possible before making a decision concerning the health, education, and welfare of the child;
(3) of access to medical, dental, psychological, and educational records of the child;
(4) to consult with a physician, dentist, or psychologist of the child;
(5) to consult with school officials concerning the child's welfare and educational status, including school activities;
(6) to attend school activities;
(7) to be designated on the child 's records as a person to be notified in case of an emergency;
(8) to consent to medical, dental, and surgical treatment during an emergency involving an immediate danger to the health and safety of the child; and
(9) to manage the estate of the child to the extent the estate has been created by the parent or the parent's family.

Unless limited by court order, a parent appointed as a conservator of a child has the following rights and duties during the period that the parent has possession of the child:
(1) the duty of care, control, protection, and reasonable discipline of the child;
(2) the duty to support the child, including providing the child with clothing, food, shelter, and medical and dental care not involving an invasive procedure;
(3) the right to consent for the child to medical and dental care not involving an invasive procedure; and
(4) the right to direct the moral and religious training of the child.
                    -From Section 153.073 and 153.074 of the Texas Family Code.

Rights of Sole Managing Conservator.
Unless limited by court order, a parent appointed as sole managing conservator of a child has the rights and duties listed above, as well as the following exclusive rights:
(1) the right to designate the primary residence of the child;
(2) the right to consent to medical, dental, and surgical treatment involving invasive procedures;
(3) the right to consent to psychiatric and psychological treatment;
(4) the right to receive and give receipt for periodic payments for the support of the child and to hold or disburse these funds for the benefit of the child;
(5) the right to represent the child in legal action and to make other decisions of substantial legal significance concerning the child;
(6) the right to consent to marriage and to enlistment in the armed forces of the United States;
(7) the right to make decisions concerning the child's education;
(8) the right to the services and earnings of the child; and
(9) except when a guardian of the child 's estate or a guardian or attorney ad litem has been appointed for the child, the right to act as an agent of the child in relation to the child's estate if the child 's action is required by a state, the United States, or a foreign government.
                    -From Section 153.132 of the Texas Family Code.

Utah

Child Custody Guidelines.

Utah laws allow the court to make an order for the future care and custody of the parties' minor children as it considers appropriate. The court shall consider the best interests of the child and, among other factors the court finds relevant, the following:

(a) whether the physical, psychological, and emotional needs and development of the child will benefit from joint legal or physical custody;

(b) the ability of the parents to give first priority to the welfare of the child and reach shared decisions in the child's best interest;

(c) whether each parent is capable of encouraging and accepting a positive relationship between the child and the other parent, including the sharing of love, affection, and contact between the child and the other parent;

(d) whether both parents participated in raising the child before the divorce;

(e) the geographical proximity of the homes of the parents;

(f) the preference of the child if the child is of sufficient age and capacity to reason so as to form an intelligent preference as to joint legal or physical custody;

(g) the maturity of the parents and their willingness and ability to protect the child from conflict that may arise between the parents;

(h) the past and present ability of the parents to cooperate with each other and make decisions jointly;

(i) any history of, or potential for, child abuse, spouse abuse, or kidnapping;

(j) the past conduct and demonstrated moral standards of each of the parties;

(k) which parent is most likely to act in the best interest of the child, including allowing the child frequent and continuing contact with the noncustodial parent; and

(l) any other factors the court finds relevant.

The court shall, in every case, consider joint custody but may award any form of custody which is determined to be in the best interest of the child. When deciding whether to award joint custody, the court will consider the same factors as above.

The court may take into consideration the children's desires for custody, but the expressed desires are not controlling and the court may determine the children's custody or parent-time otherwise. The desires of a child 16 years of age or older shall be given added weight, but is not the single controlling factor.

-From 3-3-10 of the Utah Statutes.

Definitions.

"Joint legal custody" means the sharing of the rights, privileges, duties, and powers of a parent by both parents, where specified, and may include an award of exclusive authority by the court to one parent to make specific decisions. The court can award joint legal custody and still award sole physical custody to one parent.

"Joint physical custody" means the child stays with each parent overnight for more than 30% of the year, and both parents contribute to the expenses of the child in addition to paying child support. A court may still designate one parent as the primary caretaker and one home as the primary residence of the child.

-From 30-3-10.1 & 10.2 of the Utah Statutes.

Moving with the Child.
When either parent decides to move out of state, or at least 150 miles from their current residence, that parent shall provide 60 days advance written notice of the intended relocation to the other parent, if possible.

The court has a specific minimum visitation schedule that must be followed even when the parent relocates, unless the court orders otherwise.

The court may, upon motion of any party or upon the court's own motion, schedule a hearing to review the notice of relocation and parent-time schedule, and to make appropriate orders regarding the parent-time and costs for parent-time transportation.

In determining the parent-time schedule and allocating the transportation costs, the court shall consider:
(a) the reason for the parent's relocation;
(b) the additional costs or difficulty to both parents in exercising
    parent-time;
(c) the economic resources of both parents; and
(d) other factors the court considers necessary and relevant.

Upon the motion of any party, the court may order the parent intending to move to pay the costs of transportation for at least one visit per year with the other parent, and any number of additional visits as determined equitable by the court.

-From 30-3-37 of the Utah Statutes.

Vermont
Definitions.
"Parental rights and responsibilities" means the rights and responsibilities related to a child's physical living arrangements, parent child contact, education, medical and dental care, religion, travel and any other matter involving a child's welfare and upbringing.

"Legal responsibility" means the rights and responsibilities to determine and control various matters affecting a child's welfare and upbringing, other than routine daily care and control of the child. These matters include but are not limited to education, medical and dental care, religion and travel arrangements. Legal responsibility may be held solely or may be divided or shared.

"Physical responsibility" means the rights and responsibilities to provide routine daily care and control of the child subject to the right of the other parent to have contact with the child. Physical responsibility may be held solely or may be divided or shared.

-From § 664 of the Vermont Statutes.

Child Custody Guidelines.
The court will only order joint legal custody if the parents agree on joint legal custody. In awarding child custody, Vermont laws require the court to be guided by the best interests of the child, and to consider at least the following factors:
(1) the relationship of the child with each parent and the ability and disposition of each parent to provide the child with love, affection and guidance;
(2) the ability and disposition of each parent to assure that the child receives adequate food, clothing, medical care, other material needs and a safe environment;
(3) the ability and disposition of each parent to meet the child's present and future developmental needs;
(4) the quality of the child's adjustment to the child's present housing, school and community and the potential effect of any change;
(5) the ability and disposition of each parent to foster a positive relationship and frequent and continuing contact with the other parent, including physical contact, except where contact will result in harm to the child or to a parent;
(6) the quality of the child's relationship with the primary care provider, if appropriate given the child's age and development;
(7) the relationship of the child with any other person who may significantly affect the child;
(8) the ability and disposition of the parents to communicate, cooperate with each other and make joint decisions concerning the children where parental rights and responsibilities are to be shared or divided; and
(9) evidence of abuse, and the impact of the abuse on the child and on the relationship between the child and the abusing parent.
The court shall not apply a preference for one parent over the other because of the sex of the child, the sex of a parent or the financial resources of a parent.
-From § 665 of the Vermont Statutes.

Parenting Agreement.
Any agreement between the parents which divides or shares parental rights and responsibilities shall be presumed to be in the best interests of the child. An agreement between the parties which is a complete agreement on parental rights and responsibilities shall include provisions that address at least the following:
(1) physical living arrangements;
(2) parent child contact;
(3) education of the minor child;
(4) medical, dental and health care;
(5) travel arrangements;
(6) procedures for communicating about the child's welfare; and
(7) if parental rights and responsibilities are to be shared or divided, procedures for resolving disputes. Such procedures may include but shall not be limited to mediation and binding arbitration.
-From § 666 of the Vermont Statutes.

Virginia

16.1-278.15. Custody or visitation, child or spousal support generally.

A. In cases involving the custody, visitation or support of a child pursuant to subdivision A 3 of § 16.1-241, the court may make any order of disposition to protect the welfare of the child and family as may be made by the circuit court. The parties to any petition where a child whose custody, visitation, or support is contested shall show proof that they have attended within the 12 months prior to their court appearance or that they shall attend within 45 days thereafter an educational seminar or other like program conducted by a qualified person or organization approved by the court. The court may require the parties to attend such seminar or program in uncontested cases only if the court finds good cause. The seminar or other program shall be a minimum of four hours in length and shall address the effects of separation or divorce on children, parenting responsibilities, options for conflict resolution and financial responsibilities. Once a party has completed one educational seminar or other like program, the required completion of additional programs shall be at the court's discretion. Parties under this section shall include natural or adoptive parents of the child, or any person with a legitimate interest as defined in § 20-124.1. The fee charged a party for participation in such program shall be based on the party's ability to pay; however, no fee in excess of $50 may be charged. Whenever possible, before participating in mediation or alternative dispute resolution to address custody, visitation or support, each party shall have attended the educational seminar or other like program. The court may grant an exemption from attendance of such program for good cause shown or if there is no program reasonably available. Other than statements or admissions by a party admitting criminal activity or child abuse or neglect, no statement or admission by a party in such seminar or program shall be admissible into evidence in any subsequent proceeding. If support is ordered for a child, the order shall also provide that support will continue to be paid for a child over the age of 18 who is (i) a full-time high school student, (ii) not self-supporting, and (iii) living in the home of the parent seeking or receiving child support, until the child reaches the age of 19 or graduates from high school, whichever occurs first. The court may also order the continuation of support for any child over the age of 18 who is (a) severely and permanently mentally or physically disabled, (b) unable to live independently and support himself, and (c) resides in the home of the parent seeking or receiving child support.

B. In any case involving the custody or visitation of a child, the court may award custody upon petition to any party with a legitimate interest therein, including, but not limited to, grandparents, stepparents, former stepparents, blood relatives and family members. The term "legitimate interest" shall be broadly construed to accommodate the best interest of the child. The authority of the juvenile court to consider a petition involving the custody of a child shall not be proscribed or limited where the custody of the child has previously been awarded to a local board of social services.

C. In any determination of support obligation under this section, the support obligation as it becomes due and unpaid creates a judgment by operation of law. Such judgment becomes a lien against real estate only when docketed in the county or city where such real estate is located. Nothing herein shall be construed to alter or amend the process of attachment of any lien on personal property.

D. Orders entered prior to July 1, 2008, shall not be deemed void or voidable solely because the petition or motion that resulted in the order was completed, signed and filed by a nonattorney employee of the Department of Social Services.

E. In cases involving charges for desertion, abandonment or failure to provide support by any person in violation of law, disposition shall be made in accordance with Chapter 5 (§ 20-61 et seq.) of Title 20.

F. In cases involving a spouse who seeks spousal support after having separated from his spouse, the court may enter any appropriate order to protect the welfare of the spouse seeking support.

G. In any case or proceeding involving the custody or visitation of a child, the court shall consider the best interest of the child, including the considerations for determining custody and visitation set forth in Chapter 6.1 (§ 20-124.1 et seq.) of Title 20.

H. In any proceeding before the court for custody or visitation of a child, the court may order a custody or a psychological evaluation of any parent, guardian, legal custodian or person standing in loco parentis to the child, if the court finds such evaluation would assist it in its determination. The court may enter such orders as it deems appropriate for the payment of the costs of the evaluation by the parties.

I. When deemed appropriate by the court in any custody or visitation matter, the court may order drug testing of any parent, guardian, legal custodian or person standing in loco parentis to the child. The court may enter such orders as it deems appropriate for the payment of the costs of the testing by the parties.

(1991, c. 534; 1992, cc. 585, 716, 742; 1994, c. 769; 1996, cc. 767, 879, 884; 2000, c. 586; 2002, c. 300; 2003, cc. 31, 45; 2004, c. 732; 2008, cc. 136, 845.)

Washington
Parenting Plan.
(RCW 26.09.181-26.09.225)

Every divorce case involving child custody, whether uncontested or contested, must include a parenting plan that will set out provisions for resolution of future disputes between the parents, allocation of decision-making authority (legal custody), and residential provisions (physical custody) for the child.

Laws Restricting Visitation with the Child.

The court may place restrictions on a parent's visitation time with the child if it finds any of the following factors exist:

1. Willful abandonment that continues for an extended period of time or substantial refusal to perform parenting functions;
2. Physical, sexual, or a pattern of emotional abuse of a child;
3. A history of acts of domestic violence or an assault or sexual assault which causes grievous bodily harm or the fear of such harm.
4. A parent's neglect or substantial nonperformance of parenting functions;
5. A long-term emotional or physical impairment which interferes with the parent's performance of parenting functions as defined in RCW 26.09.004;
6. A long-term impairment resulting from drug, alcohol, or other substance abuse that interferes with the performance of parenting functions;
7. The absence or substantial impairment of emotional ties between the parent and the child;

8. The abusive use of conflict by the parent which creates the danger of serious damage to the child's psychological development;

9. A parent has withheld from the other parent access to the child for a protracted period without good cause; or

10. Such other factors or conduct as the court expressly finds adverse to the best interests of the child.

Legal Custody Guidelines.

Assuming none of the following factors exist, the court will allocate decision-making authority (legal custody) to one or both parties regarding the children's education, health care, and religious upbringing based on the parenting plan proposed by the parents. Regardless of the allocation of decision-making in the parenting plan, either parent may make emergency decisions affecting the health or safety of the child. Each parent also may make decisions regarding the day-to-day care and control of the child while the child is residing with that parent.

The court shall consider the following in deciding whether to award in favor of or against joint legal custody:

1. The history of participation of each parent in decision making regarding the child(ren);

2. Whether the parents have a demonstrated ability and desire to cooperate with one another in making decisions regarding the child(ren);

3. The parents' geographic proximity to one another, to the extent that it affects their ability to make timely mutual decisions.

Physical Custody Guidelines.

The court shall make residential provisions for each child which encourage each parent to maintain a loving, stable, and nurturing relationship with the child, consistent with the child's developmental level and the family's social and economic circumstances. The court shall consider the following factors when determining the residential custody of the child:

1. The relative strength, nature, and stability of the child's relationship with each parent, including whether a parent has taken greater responsibility for performing parenting functions relating to the daily needs of the child;

2. The agreements of the parties, provided they were entered into knowingly and voluntarily;

3. Each parent's past and potential for future performance of parenting functions;

4. The emotional needs and developmental level of the child;

5. The child's relationship with siblings and with other significant adults, as well as the child's involvement with his or her physical surroundings, school, or other significant activities;

6. The wishes of the parents and the wishes of a child who is sufficiently mature to express reasoned and independent preferences as to his or her residential schedule; and

7. Each parent's employment schedule, and shall make accommodations consistent with those schedules.

Joint Physical Custody.
The court may order that a child frequently alternate his or her residence between the households of the parents for brief and substantially equal intervals of time (joint physical custody) only if the court finds the following:
1. The parties have agreed to such provisions and the agreement was knowingly and voluntarily entered into; or
2. The parties have a satisfactory history of cooperation and shared performance of parenting functions; the parties are available to each other, especially in geographic proximity, to the extent necessary to ensure their ability to share performance of the parenting functions; and the provisions are in the best interests of the child.

Access to Records.
Each parent shall have full and equal access to the education and health care records of the child absent a court order to the contrary. Neither parent may veto the access requested by the other parent.

Washington, D.C.
Custody of children.
§ 16-914.
(a)(1)(A) In any proceeding between parents in which the custody of a child is raised as an issue, the best interest of the child shall be the primary consideration. The race, color, national origin, political affiliation, sex, sexual orientation, or gender identity or expression of a party, in and of itself, shall not be a conclusive consideration. The Court shall make a determination as to the legal custody and the physical custody of a child. A custody order may include:
(i) sole legal custody;
(ii) sole physical custody;
(iii) joint legal custody;
(iv) joint physical custody; or
(v) any other custody arrangement the Court may determine is in the best interest of the child.
(B) For the purposes of this paragraph, the term:
(i) "Legal custody" means legal responsibility for a child. The term "legal custody" includes the right to make decisions regarding that child's health, education, and general welfare, the right to access the child's educational, medical, psychological, dental, or other records, and the right to speak with and obtain information regarding the child from school officials, health care providers, counselors, or other persons interacting with the child.
(ii) "Physical custody" means a child's living arrangements. The term "physical custody" includes a child's residency or visitation schedule.
(2) Unless the court determines that it is not in the best interest of the child, the court may issue an order that provides for frequent and continuing contact between each parent and the minor child or children and for the sharing of responsibilities of child-rearing and encouraging the love, affection, and contact between the minor child or children and the parents regardless of marital status. There shall be a rebuttable presumption that joint custody is in the best interest of the

child or children, except in instances where a judicial officer has found by a preponderance of the evidence that an intrafamily offense as defined in D.C. Official Code section 16-1001(5), an instance of child abuse as defined in section
102 of the Prevention of Child Abuse and Neglect Act of 1977, effective September 23, 1977 (D.C. Law 2-22; D.C. Official Code § 4-1301.02), an instance
of child neglect as defined in section 2 of the Child Abuse and Neglect Prevention Children's Trust Fund Act of 1993, effective October 5, 1993 (D.C. Law 10-
56; D.C. Official Code § 4-1341.01), or where parental kidnapping as defined in
D.C. Official Code section 16-1021 through section 16-1026 has occurred.
There shall be a rebuttable presumption that joint custody is not in the best interest of the child or children if a judicial officer finds by a preponderance of the
evidence that an intrafamily offense as defined in D.C. Official Code section 16-
1001(5), an instance of child abuse as defined in section 102 of the Prevention
of Child Abuse and Neglect Act of 1977, effective September 23, 1977 (D.C.
Law 2-22; D.C. Official Code § 4-1301.02), an instance of child neglect as defined in section 2 of the Child Abuse and Neglect Prevention Children's Trust
Fund Act of 1993, effective October 5, 1993 (D.C. Law 10-56; D.C. Official
Code § 4-1341.01), or where parental kidnapping as defined in D.C. Official
Code section 16-1021 through section 16-1026 has occurred.

(3) In determining the care and custody of a child, the best interest of the child shall
be the primary consideration. To determine the best interest of the child, the
court shall consider all relevant factors, including, but not limited to:

(A) the wishes of the child as to his or her custodian, where practicable;

(B) the wishes of the child's parent or parents as to the child's custody;

(C) the interaction and interrelationship of the child with his or her parent or parents,
his or her siblings, and any other person who may emotionally or psychologically affect the child's best interest;

(D) the child's adjustment to his or her home, school, and community;

(E) the mental and physical health of all individuals involved;

(F) evidence of an intrafamily offense as defined in section 16-
1001(5);

(G) the capacity of the parents to communicate and reach shared decisions affecting
the child's welfare;

(H) the willingness of the parents to share custody;

(I) the prior involvement of each parent in the child's life;

(J) the potential disruption of the child's social and school life;

(K) the geographic proximity of the parental homes as this relates to the practical
considerations of the child's residential schedule;

(L) the demands of parental employment;

(M) the age and number of children;

(N) the sincerity of each parent's request;

(O) the parent's ability to financially support a joint custody arrange
ment;

(P) the impact on Temporary Assistance for Needy Families, or Program on Work,
Employment, and Responsibilities, and medical assistance; and

(Q) the benefit to the parents.

(a-1) For the purposes of this section, if the judicial officer finds by a preponderance of evidence that a contestant for custody has committed an intrafamily offense, any determination that custody or visitation is to be granted to the abusive parent shall be supported by a written statement by the judicial officer specifying factors and findings which support that determination. In determining visitation arrangements, if the judicial officer finds that an intrafamily offense has occurred, the judicial officer shall only award visitation if the judicial officer finds that the child and custodial parent can be adequately protected from harm inflicted by the other party. The party found to have committed an intrafamily offense has the burden of proving that visitation will not endanger the child or significantly impair the child's emotional development.

(a-2) Repealed.

(b) Notice of a custody proceeding shall be given to the child's parents, guardian, or other custodian. The court, upon a showing of good cause, may permit intervention by any interested party.

(c) In any custody proceeding under this chapter, the Court may order each parent to submit a detailed parenting plan which shall delineate each parent's position with respect to the scheduling and allocation of rights and responsibilities that will best serve the interest of the minor child or children. The parenting plan may include, but shall not be limited to, provisions for:

    (1) the residence of the child or children;

    (2) the financial support based on the needs of the child and the actual resources of the parent;

    (3) visitation;

    (4) holidays, birthdays, and vacation visitation;

    (5) transportation of the child between the residences;

    (6) education;

    (7) religious training, if any;

    (8) access to the child's educational, medical, psychiatric, and dental treatment records;

    (9) except in emergencies, the responsibility for medical, psychiatric, and dental treatment decisions;

    (10) communication between the child and the parents; and

    (11) the resolution of conflict, such as a recognized family counseling or mediation service, before application to the Court to resolve a conflict.

(d) In making its custody determination, the Court:

    (1) shall consider the parenting plans submitted by the parents in evaluating the factors set forth in subsection (a)(3) of this section in fashioning a custody order;

    (2) shall designate the parent(s) who will make the major decisions concerning the health, safety, and welfare of the child that need immediate attention; and

    (3) may order either or both parents to attend parenting classes.

(e) Joint custody shall not eliminate the responsibility for child support in accordance with the applicable child support guideline as set forth in section 16-916.01.

(f)(1) An award of custody may be modified or terminated upon the motion of one or both parents, or on the Court's own motion, upon a determination that there has been a substantial and material change in circumstances and that the modification or termination is in the best interest of the child.

(2) When a motion to modify custody is filed, the burden of proof is on the party seeking a change, and the standard of proof shall be by a preponderance of the evidence.

(3) The provisions of this chapter shall apply to motions to modify or terminate any award of custody filed after April 18, 1996.

(g) The Court, for good cause and upon its own motion, may appoint a guardian ad litem or an attorney, or both, to represent the minor child's interests.

(h) The Court shall enter an order for any custody arrangement that is agreed to by both parents unless clear and convincing evidence indicates that the arrangement is not in the best interest of the minor child.

(i) An objection by one parent to any custody arrangement shall not be the sole basis for refusing the entry of an order that the Court determines is in the best interest of the minor child.

(j) The Court shall place on the record the specific factors and findings which justify any custody arrangement not agreed to by both parents.

West Virginia
§48-9-101. Scope of article; legislative findings and declarations.
(a) This article sets forth principles governing the allocation of custodial and decision-making responsibility for a minor child when the parents do not live together.

(b) The Legislature finds and declares that it is the public policy of this state to assure that the best interest of children is the court's primary concern in allocating custodial and decision-making responsibilities between parents who do not live together. In furtherance of this policy, the Legislature declares that a child's best interest will be served by assuring that minor children have frequent and continuing contact with parents who have shown the ability to act in the best interest of their children, to educate parents on their rights and responsibilities and the effect their separation may have on children, to encourage mediation of disputes, and to encourage parents to share in the rights and responsibilities of rearing their children after the parents have separated or divorced.

§48-9-102. Objectives; best interests of the child.
(a) The primary objective of this article is to serve the child's best interests, by facilitating:

(1) Stability of the child;

(2) Parental planning and agreement about the child's custodial arrangements and upbringing;

(3) Continuity of existing parent-child attachments;

(4) Meaningful contact between a child and each parent;

(5) Caretaking relationships by adults who love the child, know how to provide for the child's needs, and who place a high priority on doing so;

(6) Security from exposure to physical or emotional harm; and
(7) Expeditious, predictable decision-making and avoidance of prolonged uncertainty respecting arrangements for the child's care and control.
(b) A secondary objective of article is to achieve fairness between the parents.

§48-9-103. Parties to an action under this article.

(a) Persons who have a right to be notified of and participate as a party in an action filed by another are:
(1) A legal parent of the child, as defined in section 1-232 of this chapter;
(2) An adult allocated custodial responsibility or decision-making responsibility under a parenting plan regarding the child that is then in effect; or
(3) Persons who were parties to a prior order establishing custody and visitation, or who, under a parenting plan, were allocated custodial responsibility or decision-making responsibility.
(b) In exceptional cases the court may, in its discretion, grant permission to intervene to other persons or public agencies whose participation in the proceedings under this article it determines is likely to serve the child's best interests. The court may place limitations on participation by the intervening party as the court determines to be appropriate. Such persons or public agencies do not have standing to initiate an action under this article.

§48-9-104. Parent education classes.

(a) The family court shall, by order, and with the approval of the supreme court of appeals, designate an organization or agency to establish and operate education programs designed for parents who have filed an action for divorce, paternity, support, separate maintenance or other custody proceeding and who have minor children. The education programs shall be designed to instruct and educate parents about the effects of divorce and custody disputes on their children and to teach parents ways to help their children and minimize their trauma.
(b) The family court shall issue an order requiring parties to an action for divorce involving a minor child or children to attend parent education classes established pursuant to subsection (a) of this section unless the court determines that attendance is not appropriate or necessary based on the conduct or circumstances of the parties. The court may, by order, establish sanctions for failure to attend. The court may also order parties to an action involving paternity, separate maintenance or modification of a divorce decree to attend such classes.
(c) The family court may require that each person attending a parent education class pay a fee, not to exceed twenty-five dollars, to the clerk of the circuit court to defray the cost of materials and of hiring teachers: *Provided*, That where it is determined that a party is indigent and unable to pay for such classes, the court shall waive the payment of the fee for such party. The clerk of the circuit court shall, on or before the tenth day of each month, transmit all fees collected under this subsection to the state treasurer for deposit in the state treasury to the credit of special revenue fund to be known as the "parent education fund" which is hereby created. All moneys collected and received under this subsection and paid into the state treasury and credited to the parent education fund shall be used by the administrative office of the supreme court of appeals solely for reimbursing the provider of parent education

classes for the costs of materials and of providing such classes. Such moneys shall not be treated by the auditor and treasurer as part of the general revenue of the state.
(d) The administrative office of the supreme court of appeals shall submit a report to the joint committee on government and finance summarizing the effectiveness of any program of parent education no later than two years from the initiation of the program.

§48-9-201. Parenting agreements.
(a) If the parents agree to one or more provisions of a parenting plan, the court shall so order, unless it makes specific findings that:
(1) The agreement is not knowing or voluntary; or
(2) The plan would be harmful to the child.
(b) The court, at its discretion and on any basis it deems sufficient, may conduct an evidentiary hearing to determine whether there is a factual basis for a finding under subdivision (1) or (2), subsection (a) of this section. When there is credible information that child abuse as defined by section 49-1-3 of this code or domestic violence as defined by section 27-202 of this code has occurred, a hearing is mandatory and if the court determines that abuse has occurred, appropriate protective measures shall be ordered.
(c) If an agreement, in whole or in part, is not accepted by the court under the standards set forth in subsection (a) of this section, the court shall allow the parents the opportunity to negotiate another agreement.

§48-9-202. Court-ordered services.
(a)(1) The court shall inform the parents, or require them to be informed, about:
(A) How to prepare a parenting plan;
(B) The impact of family dissolution on children and how the needs of children facing family dissolution can best be addressed;
(C) The impact of domestic abuse on children and resources for addressing domestic abuse; and
(D) Mediation or other nonjudicial procedures designed to help them achieve an agreement.
(2) The court shall require the parents to attend parent education classes.
(3) If parents are unable to resolve issues and agree to a parenting plan, the court shall require mediation unless application of the procedural rules promulgated pursuant to the provisions of subsection (b) of this section indicates that mediation is inappropriate in the particular case.
(b) The supreme court of appeals shall make and promulgate rules that will provide for premediation screening procedures to determine whether domestic violence, child abuse or neglect, acts or threats of duress or coercion, substance abuse, mental illness or other such elements would adversely affect the safety of a party, the ability of a party to meaningfully participate in the mediation or the capacity of a party to freely and voluntarily consent to any proposed agreement reached as a result of the mediation. Such rules shall authorize a family court judge to consider alternatives to mediation which may aid the parties in establishing a parenting plan. Such rules shall not establish a per se bar to mediation if domestic violence, child abuse or neglect, acts or threats of duress or coercion, substance abuse, mental illness or other such

elements exist, but may be the basis for the court, in its discretion, not to order services under subsection (a) of this section or not to require a parent to have face-to-face meetings with the other parent.

(c) A mediator shall not make a recommendation to the court and may not reveal information that either parent has disclosed during mediation under a reasonable expectation of confidentiality, except that a mediator may reveal to the court credible information that he or she has received concerning domestic violence or child abuse.

(d) Mediation services authorized under subsection (a) of this section shall be ordered at an hourly cost that is reasonable in light of the financial circumstances of each parent, assessed on a uniform sliding scale. Where one parent's ability to pay for such services is significantly greater than the other, the court may order that parent to pay some or all of the expenses of the other. State revenues shall not be used to defray the costs for the services of a mediator: *Provided*, That the supreme court of appeals may use a portion of its budget to pay administrative costs associated with establishing and operating mediation programs: *Provided, however*, That grants and gifts to the state that may be used to fund mediation are not to be considered as state revenues for purposes of this subsection.

(e) The supreme court of appeals shall establish standards for the qualification and training of mediators.

§48-9-401. Modification upon showing of changed circumstances or harm.

(a) Except as provided in section 9-402 or 9-403, a court shall modify a parenting plan order if it finds, on the basis of facts that were not known or have arisen since the entry of the prior order and were not anticipated therein, that a substantial change has occurred in the circumstances of the child or of one or both parents and a modification is necessary to serve the best interests of the child.

(b) In exceptional circumstances, a court may modify a parenting plan if it finds that the plan is not working as contemplated and in some specific way is manifestly harmful to the child, even if a substantial change of circumstances has not occurred.

(c) Unless the parents have agreed otherwise, the following circumstances do not justify a significant modification of a parenting plan except where harm to the child is shown:

(1) Circumstances resulting in an involuntary loss of income, by loss of employment or otherwise, affecting the parent's economic status;

(2) A parent's remarriage or cohabitation; and

(3) Choice of reasonable caretaking arrangements for the child by a legal parent, including the child's placement in day care.

(d) For purposes of subsection (a) of this section, the occurrence or worsening of a limiting factor, as defined in subsection (a), section 9-209, after a parenting plan has been ordered by the court, constitutes a substantial change of circumstances and measures shall be ordered pursuant to section 9-209 to protect the child or the child's parent.

Wisconsin
Definitions.

"Joint legal custody" means the condition under which both parties share legal custody and neither party's legal custody rights are superior, except with respect to specified decisions as set forth by the court or the parties in the final judgment or order.

"Legal custody" means the right and responsibility to make major decisions concerning the child, except with respect to specified decisions as set forth by the court or the parties in the final judgment or order.

"Major decisions" include, but are not limited to, decisions regarding consent to marry, consent to enter military service, consent to obtain a motor vehicle operator's license, authorization for nonemergency health care and choice of school and religion.
-From 767.001(1s) of the Wisconsin Statutes.

Child Custody Guidelines.
Wisconsin laws require the court to consider all facts relevant to the best interest of the child, when determining child custody. The court may not prefer one parent or potential custodian over the other on the basis of the sex or race of the parent or potential custodian. The court shall consider the following factors in making its determination:

1. The wishes of the child's parent or parents, as shown by any stipulation between the parties, any proposed parenting plan or any legal custody or physical placement proposal submitted to the court at trial.
2. The wishes of the child, which may be communicated by the child or through the child's guardian ad litem or other appropriate professional.
3. The interaction and interrelationship of the child with his or her parent or parents, siblings, and any other person who may significantly affect the child's best interest.
4. The amount and quality of time that each parent has spent with the child in the past, any necessary changes to the parents' custodial roles and any reasonable lifestyle changes that a parent proposes to make to be able to spend time with the child in the future.
5. The child's adjustment to the home, school, religion and community.
6. The age of the child and the child's developmental and educational needs at different ages.
7. Whether the mental or physical health of a party, minor child, or other person living in a proposed custodial household negatively affects the child's intellectual, physical, or emotional well-being.
8. The need for regularly occurring and meaningful periods of physical placement to provide predictability and stability for the child.
9. The availability of public or private child care services.
10. The cooperation and communication between the parties and whether either party unreasonably refuses to cooperate or communicate with the other party.
11. Whether each party can support the other party's relationship with the child, including encouraging and facilitating frequent and continuing contact with the child, or whether one party is likely to unreasonably interfere with the child's continuing relationship with the other party.
12. Whether there is evidence that a party engaged in abuse of the child

13. Whether there is evidence of interspousal battery or domestic abuse
14. Whether either party has or had a significant problem with alcohol
    or drug abuse.
15. The reports of appropriate professionals if admitted into evidence.
16. Such other factors as the court may in each individual case deter
    mine to be relevant.

If the court finds that a parent has engaged in a pattern or serious incident of
interspousal battery, or domestic abuse, the safety and well-being of the child and the
safety of the parent who was the victim of the battery or abuse shall be the paramount concerns in determining legal custody and periods of physical placement.
                                    -From 767.24(5)(am) of the Wisconsin Statutes.

Wyoming
Custody and Visitation
20-2-201. Disposition and maintenance of children in decree or order; access to
records.
(a) In granting a divorce, separation or annulment of a marriage or upon the estab-
    lishment of paternity pursuant to W.S. 14-2-401 through 14-2-907, the court
    may make by decree or order any disposition of the children that appears most
    expedient and in the best interests of the children.

Best Interests of the Child
In determining the best interests of the child, the court shall consider, but is not
limited to, the following factors:
(i) The quality of the relationship each child has with each parent;
(ii) The ability of each parent to provide adequate care for each child throughout
    each period of responsibility, including arranging for each child's care by others
    as needed;
(iii) The relative competency and fitness of each parent;
(iv) Each parent's willingness to accept all responsibilities of parenting, including a
    willingness to accept care for each child at specified times and to relinquish care
    to the other parent at specified times;
(v) How the parents and each child can best maintain and strengthen a relationship
    with each other;
(vi) How the parents and each child interact and communicate with each other and
    how such interaction and communication may be improved;
(vii) The ability and willingness of each parent to allow the other to provide care
    without intrusion, respect the other parent's rights and responsibilities, includ-
    ing the right to privacy;
(viii) Geographic distance between the parents' residences;
(ix) The current physical and mental ability of each parent to care for each child;
(x) Any other factors the court deems necessary and relevant.
(b) In any proceeding in which the custody of a child is at issue the court shall not
    prefer one (1) parent as a custodian solely because of gender.
(c) The court shall consider evidence of spousal abuse or child abuse as being
    contrary to the best interest of the children. If the court finds that family vio-

lence has occurred, the court shall make arrangements for visitation that best protects the children and the abused spouse from further harm.

(d) The court shall order custody in well defined terms to promote understanding and compliance by the parties. Custody shall be crafted to promote the best interests of the children, and may include any combination of joint, shared or sole custody.

(e) Unless otherwise ordered by the court, the noncustodial parent shall have the same right of access as the parent awarded custody to any records relating to the child of the parties, including school records, activities, teachers and teachers' conferences as well as medical and dental treatment providers and mental health records.

(f) At any time the court may require parents to attend appropriate parenting classes, including but not limited to, parenting classes to lessen the effects of divorce on children.

20-2-202.

Visitation.

(a) The court may order visitation it deems in the best interests of each child and the court shall:

(i) Order visitation in enough detail to promote understanding and compliance;

(ii) Provide for the allocation of the costs of transporting each child for purposes of visitation;

(iii) Require either parent who plans to change their home city or state of residence, to give written notice thirty (30) days prior to the move, both to the other parent and to the clerk of district court stating the date and destination of the move.

Jurisdiction for enforcement and modification.

(a) A court in this state which enters a custody order under W.S. 20-2-201 has continuing subject matter jurisdiction to enforce or modify the decree concerning the care, custody and visitation of the children as the circumstances of the parents and needs of the child require, subject to the provisions of the Uniform Child Custody Jurisdiction and Enforcement Act. A court which has jurisdiction to enforce or modify an order under this section may decline to exercise its jurisdiction if it finds it is an inconvenient forum under the circumstances of the case and that the court which entered the original order is a more appropriate forum and has jurisdiction as set forth in the Uniform Child Custody Jurisdiction and Enforcement Act.

(b) A court in any county in Wyoming in which the child has lived with his parents, a parent or a person acting as a parent for six (6) consecutive months immediately prior to commencement of the custody proceeding may assert subject matter jurisdiction and adjudicate any proceedings involving the child. Periods of temporary absence of any of the named persons shall be included as part of the six (6) month period.

(c) Any party seeking to enforce or modify a custody order pursuant to this section shall attach a certified copy of the custody order to the petition to be enforced or modified. A certified copy of an order entered by a Wyoming court providing for the care, custody or visitation of children may be filed in the office of the clerk of the district court of any county in this state in which either parent resides if neither parent resides in the county of original jurisdiction. The district court for the county in which the order is filed has jurisdiction to enforce the order, provided:

(i) Upon request of the district court for the county in which a certified copy of the order has been filed, the court which originally entered the order shall forward certified copies of the transcript of the court record and pleadings, orders, decrees, records of hearings, social studies and other pertinent documents relating to the original proceeding; and

(ii) The district court for the county in which a certified copy of the order has been filed shall give due consideration to the transcript of the record and all other documents submitted to it in accordance with paragraph (i) of this subsection.

(d) In any proceeding to enforce or modify an order concerning the care, custody and visitation of children, any required notice or pleading shall be served as provided by the Wyoming Rules of Civil Procedure.

Enforcement and modification.
20-2-204.

(a) Either parent may petition to enforce or modify any court order regarding custody and visitation.

(b) A court having jurisdiction under W.S. 20-2-203 may, upon appropriate motion of a party, require a parent to appear before the court and show just cause why the parent should not be held in contempt, upon a showing that the parent has willfully violated an order concerning the care, custody and visitation of the children. In order to enforce and require future compliance with an order the court may find that the parent is in contempt of court, award attorney's fees, costs and any other relief as the court may deem necessary under the circumstances to the party aggrieved by the violation of an order.

(c) A court having jurisdiction may modify an order concerning the care, custody and visitation of the children if there is a showing by either parent of a material change in circumstances since the entry of the order in question and that the modification would be in the best interests of the children pursuant to W.S. 20-2-201(a). In any proceeding in which a parent seeks to modify an order concerning child custody or visitation, proof of repeated, unreasonable failure by the custodial parent to allow visitation to the other parent in violation of an order may be considered as evidence of a material change of circumstances.

APPENDIX J: DO *SOMETHING* CHALLENGE

1) Locate your state representatives at:
   http://www.frc.org/elected-officials

2) Type or handwrite a letter about the family law(s) you want changed. If needed, use the example on the following page.

3) Make your letter simple, short, and readable. Be sure to include the exact law(s) you want changed.

4) Copy or scan the letter and stamped envelope before mailing.

5) You can email scanned copies to: clay@mdpsg.com; or you can mail the copies to:

   MDPSG
   PO BOX 888865
   Atlanta, Georgia 30356
   United States

6) **Since I might publish your letter**, DO NOT include private information in the letter that you would not want others to see.

7) If I publish your letter, I will not include your *full* contact information: *only* your first, last name, city, and state.

8) There is a form that I need you to include. Get the form at: www.honestguides.com/childcustody.htm

Letter Example Below

Clay H. Emerton
3255 Dallas Hwy
Marietta, Georgia 30152
clay@mdpsg.com

May 20, 2009

Sen. Saxby Chambliss
100 Galleria, Suite 1340
Atlanta, Georgia 30339

Senator Chambliss:

I am writing to request that you initiate and support the REFORM of *child custody legislation* in our state and **nation-wide**.

I AM REQUESTING A "SHARED PARENTING PRESUMPTION" FOR TYPICAL DIVORCING PARENTS.

The "Shared Parenting Presumption" should include:
1) TWO CUSTODIAL PARENTS
If both parents agree to maintain residence in/near a child's school district at the time of the divorce filing, parents should share not only legal custody, but 50/50 PHYSICAL custody. Both parents should be mandated to use an <u>affordable</u> mediator when parenting disagreements cannot be resolved. A preferred mediator should be identified in the divorce agreement.

2) SIMPLIFICATION OF CUSTODY CHANGES
Simplification should involve the submission of a basic court document and then the completion of a structured assessment from a private, licensed family professional. Changes in custody should be simple and affordable for any parent showing an active interest.

3) PROTECTION FROM RELOCATION OF CHILDREN

Parents who are participating in "Shared Parenting" cannot relocate a child from a school district without the other parent moving also. All relocations from the current school district should be together as a family, or not at all.

4) NO CHILD SUPPORT

Parents who participate in "Shared Parenting" should be protected from paying child support. Instead, courts should *liberalize temporary* **alimony** payments when necessary. When child support is necessary, it should be presumed to be temporary until shared parenting can be recommended by a family professional.

Respectfully,

Clay H. Emerton #   ##

Clay H. Emerton

REFERENCES

Center for American Women in Politics. (2009). "Women in Elective Office 2009". Retrieved from http://www.cawp.rutgers.edu/fast_facts/levels_of_office/documents/elective.pdf

Fisher, H. (2004). Why we love. New York: Henry Holt

Help Yourself Divorce. (2008). "State Divorce Laws". Retrieved from http://www.helpyourselfdivorce.com/articles_list.html.

Rogers, C. (1961) *On becoming a person: a therapist's view of psychotherapy.* Boston: Houghton Mifflin.

Wallerstein, J. S., Lewis, J. M., Blakeslee, S. (2000). *The unexpected legacy of divorce.* New York: Hyperion.

ABOUT THE AUTHOR

A FATHER OF THREE

Clay Emerton is the father of two daughters and a son. He shares a 50% physical custody schedule with the children's mother, Shauna.

The family currently resides in North Atlanta, Georgia, in the same school district of course. Clay and Shauna are negotiating his desire for the family to relocate to Tampa, Florida. The entire family will remain comfortably in Atlanta until a move is considered fair to both parents.

FOUNDER & PRESIDENT OF *PARENT ROAD*

Clay is the President and Founder of Parent Road, a nonprofit parenting support organization. Beginning in 2005, Clay has contributed thousands of hours designing and supporting online training courses for parents to overcome anger issues, parenting issues, and substance abuse problems.

PRESIDENT OF *MARRIAGE, DIVORCE, AND PERSONAL SERVICES GROUP*

Clay leads the Marriage, Divorce and Personal Services Group where he works to understand and resolve typical problems of modern families. At MDPSG, Clay provides online mediation and marriage counseling through video web cam conference technology. Visit MDPSG.com for more details.

EDUCATION AND TRAINING

Clay has a Bachelor of Science degree in Human Resources Development from Indiana State University. He is also working on his Master's Degree in Marriage and Family Therapy.

MORE BOOKS FROM CHANGE PUBLISHING

Honest Guides Limited Collection

The Honest Guide about Cheating:
Facing the Facts of Infidelity

The Honest Guide to Divorce:
Getting Your Life Back

The Honest Guide to Coparenting:
Practical Advice for Parents Already Divorced

The Honest Guide to Breakups:
Working Out of Codependency

Shocking Guides Limited Collection

The Shocking Guide to Quitting Smoking:
Psychology and Nicotine Addiction

The Shocking Guide to God and Religion:
A Workbook about Personal Spirituality

The Shocking Guide to Finding Happiness:
A Workbook about Depression and Finding Yourself

The Shocking Guide to Active Marriage:
A Workbook for Married Couples

Get yours at Amazon.com or Changepub.com!

Legislative Representative List*

PRESIDENT

The White House
President Barack Obama
District of Columbia 20500

HOUSE REPRESENTATIVE

Name: _____

Address: _____

_____

_____

U.S. SENATE

Name: _____

Address: _____

_____

_____

U.S. SENATE

Name: _____

Address: _____

_____

_____

OTHER

Name: _____

Address: _____

_____

_____

*FIND OFFICIALS: HTTP://WWW.FRC.ORG/ELECTED-OFFICIALS

Notes